MW01137988

BECOME
A SUCCESSFUL
VIRTUAL ASSISTANT

*Learn the Business Side
& Ditch 9 to 5*

Melissa Smith, The PVA

This book is dedicated to my fellow admins and virtual assistants. We've come a long way, and we have only just begun!

HOW TO USE THIS BOOK

This book is a step-by-step guide to help you learn the business side of virtual assistance and ditch your 9 to 5 job successfully. Whether you are simply thinking about making the transition or have already left your job, this book will help you get to where you want to be in the least amount of time and by spending the least amount of money.

Reading this book is only the first step. You must take action. That is why I created a workbook for you. At the end of each chapter, you will complete the assignments and journal your thoughts and progress in the workbook. No matter where you are in the process of building your business, the workbook will ask the questions that will lead you to solving problems, ultimately helping you work with your ideal clients and growing your business in the right way.

The workbook is my complimentary gift to you. You will learn everything you need to know while reading this book. However, learning and taking actionable steps are not the same. To get the most out of this book and to create the most for your business, use the workbook. Download it now so you are ready to complete each section after you read each chapter.

After you download the workbook, you'll also be added to my email list to be notified when clients are looking for virtual assistants just like you. You'll also be the first to know about free promotions, upcoming events, and news that I share only with my VA community. Basically, you'll be a part of my inner circle with plenty of access to me!

Visit www.thepva.com/complimentary-workbook/ to download the workbook, and let's get started!

TABLE OF CONTENTS

CHAPTER 3

CHAPTER 4

CHAPTER 5

CHAPTER 6

CHAPTER 7

CHAPTER 8

BONUS—BEFORE YOU GO OUT ON YOUR OWN

CONCLUSION

INTRODUCTION

Congratulations on making the decision to change your life by becoming a virtual assistant! You might have seen ads or heard of someone who was working as a VA and wondered if you could do the same. I know I did. As I began looking into the options, the most appealing one was the option of creating my own VA business. I wrote this book to teach you all you need to know to start your own VA business. By sharing my own experiences and insights, you will save months or even years trying to figure everything out on your own!

I first became a virtual assistant while working remotely for my employer. After only a few months of being a VA, my employer sent out new contracts for the year. I had to make a decision then for the upcoming year. Suddenly my lifelong philosophy of "I will never own my own business" didn't seem like such a bad idea. If I could do what I was doing for my employer, couldn't I do it for myself?

With little thought, no business plan, no knowledge of how to run a business, and—crazy enough—no fear, I sent the contract back to my employer—unsigned.

I told my employer I felt this was my opportunity, and I had to take it. It was now or never. He understood and was supportive. I finished out my contract and then I was officially on my own. There was one big problem. Where do I find my clients? The question virtual assistants ask the most, second only to "How do I get rid of this client?"

Sadly, not all VAs make it through the first year and some are never able to do more than keep it as a side gig ultimately working two jobs. Throughout this book I will answer the most asked questions, including the questions you don't know you need to ask. I will take you from where you are now to owning a successful virtual assistant business in the least amount of time, spending the least amount of money, and get you to your first client quickly. You'll learn how to grow, scale, and reach elite VA status generating income through several different sources all without being chained to a desk.

I never had a problem getting a job in my life. Somehow I thought gaining clients would be as simple. I would prove myself wrong. That one problem led to so many other questions that I couldn't answer. And I quickly realized no one could help me. All the mentors, coaches, and guides didn't understand where I was coming from. They had never been an administrative professional. They were not familiar with the mindset of an admin, so they didn't know how to transition my skills to the virtual assistance world.

Through trial and error, I learned to weave business principles into the mindset and service-based world of virtual assistance. I figured out how to do what I do best, how to get paid what I'm worth, and how to enjoy the life of being a business owner. I ditched the traditional 9 to 5 job and made my own rules. Being a VA isn't simply about doing the work of an assistant; it is understanding the business side of business.

Consider this book your roadmap. I wish someone had given me one! This roadmap will provide you a foundation on which to build your VA business. You will be able to take the principles and guides in this book and personalize them to your own business. While the process won't be linear, each step will reveal another opportunity.

I'll share what others won't tell you. They can't. They don't know. I have the unique perspective of matching clients with VAs and consulting others, answering all their questions, listening to what they are looking for and what makes a good virtual assistant. Any VA can make the minimum.

You'll learn how to get the premium clients, how to work with the best of the best. Ultimately, you'll be able to live out your wildest dreams.

My Dream

I reached my dream while walking through the Plasa de Mesina on a warm sunny day in May of 2016. All of a sudden, I started to get alerts on my phone. At first, I thought it was bad news. I was a little nervous. When I found a quiet place to check the messages, disbelief overwhelmed me and I cried tears of joy before celebrating. My book *Hire the Right Virtual Assistant*, which had been released earlier in the week, reached Amazon bestseller status.

Suddenly I had emails and connection requests not only from potential clients but from admins wanting to become VAs and VAs who were struggling to grow their businesses. They wanted to know what to do. How do they get clients? How could they survive on their own and quit their day jobs? Could it be done? I answered every single request, including conducting hundreds of meetings. When I kept getting the same questions over and over again, I was almost relieved I wasn't alone. I was so happy to share what I knew.

Soon I had a VA consulting business. No one else was sharing the information I was. To help provide the best information from the best professionals in the business, I created the Admin to VA Summit and an online course called The Essential Business Model for VAs. This book is the step-by-step guide I've used on every call, consultation, and class. I know it works not just for me but for anyone who follows the steps.

Looking back, it didn't take long to grow my business, but it was long enough for me to suffer plenty of sleepless nights, shed plenty of tears, stress myself out, and fear making the wrong decisions. I don't want you to go through this!

I have worked with, consulted, and surveyed hundreds of people who have transitioned from admins to VAs. The result is what you're reading—the most complete book on how to succeed in business as a VA, how to learn the business side of business and ditch the 9 to 5. Why would I take the time to write this book? Because it is my deep passion and desire to successfully help admins move through the challenging transition of becoming a virtual assistant. Like a Sherpa, I will guide you through a carefully mapped out process with a proven track record.

Why do you want to become a VA? Maybe you were laid off or your company went out of business. Maybe you hate your job or the commute. Or maybe you've retired from the daily grind, but you still want to use your skills in a profitable way. Even if you're at the top of your game, it all boils down to one word: Choice.

When you become a VA, the choices are all yours. It's more than freedom and flexibility, more than unlimited earning potential, more than spending your time when and how you'd like. As a virtual assistant, you get to choose the life you want to have while at the same time doing the work you love.

As a full-time employee, I was tired of choosing. I was tired of feeling guilty (even though no one made me feel that way) when I took a vacation. I was tired of choosing what to choose. My final choice was to choose me and to go out on my own.

I had no idea where the next few years would take me. One day I was given the opportunity to be location independent, allowing me to travel to 16 countries in 12 months. Again, I chose myself, my business.

This book is for those who are ready to take the step and go from an admin to a VA. Whether you are excited, nervous, scared, worried, or feel alone,

I'm here to walk you through the process. I've known all those feelings intimately. I went from struggling to make ends meet to being able to travel the world. If I can conquer an almost lifetime fear of flying, 15 years of anxiety, and swearing I would never own my own business, you can certainly have whatever you dream about too!

The purpose of this book is also to give back to the administrative field and the virtual assistant profession which has given me so much. I love it dearly and consider it my duty to help those who come after me the same way the road was paved before me, to help others achieve the same freedom and flexibility I enjoy, and to help others no longer have to make the difficult choices regarding work.

Throughout this book, I will answer the most asked questions about starting your own VA business, including the questions you don't even know to ask. I will take you from where you are now to owning a successful virtual assistant business in the least amount of time and by spending the least amount of money. I'll also explain how to find your first client quickly. You'll learn how to grow, scale, and reach elite VA status, generating income through several different sources—all without being chained to a desk. Owning your own VA business means you can do what you love, create the life you want, and get paid what you're worth. Let's get started!

Let's Start with the Basics

Depending on how long you've been an executive assistant, your idea of what an EA does will vary. I remember watching the movie *9 to 5* as a young girl and then *Working Girl* when I was a bit older. To say times have changed would be an understatement!

I remember when I left Georgia and moved back home to California. I was working in the Bay Area just over the Bay Bridge from San Francisco. I met admins who specialized in the world of tech and start-ups, a field I was extremely unfamiliar with. I decided to do what any good admin does—I joined an admin group, OrgOrg, to learn more. My fascination grew as I was finding out about the latest and greatest technologies and software. It was exhilarating to learn about the new fields of technology start-up companies.

When I went to my first OfficeNinjas event and met a virtual assistant, my mind was blown. Virtual assistants did everything remotely. They got to choose the work they performed and the hours they worked. It sounded like a dream! Except I already had my dream job with a nice salary. The other option of owning my own business wasn't alluring at the time. With no reason to leave my job and become a virtual assistant, I stayed and loved my work. Until one day I had to move back to Georgia.

As I went to my boss in tears (I *really* loved my job and the company and didn't want to move again) to give my notice, he switched things up on me and asked how they could keep me. Immediately I said, "I can do most of what I do virtually. I don't have to actually be in the office."

His response, "Okay, then. Let's do that."

Working remotely drastically changed my life. I was on the opposite side of the country working seamlessly for my employer. Turns out without all the interruptions and chats over coffee, I completed my work in less than half the time! I considered myself to be extremely efficient in the office. I had no idea I would be more productive working remotely.

With more time on my hands, I began to wonder if there was something to owning my own company. After a lifetime of saying I would never own my own business, something inside me changed. I grew up in a family that was in the restaurant business. I thought owning a business would mean I was shackled to it like my family was chained to its restaurant business. But virtual assistance seemed completely different.

Only a few months later when contracts for the next year needed to be signed for my employer, I made the decision to go out on my own. I finished out my contract and then officially became a full-time business owner.

Virtual assistants are not employees. We are business owners. Even thinking of yourself in the full-time or part-time sense is damaging to how much revenue you can bring in. Somehow working part-time translates into our minds as making less. This is simply not true.

This wasn't the only issue I faced as I made the transition from EA to VA. Because I was transitioning from an executive assistant to a virtual assistant, I decided to position myself as an executive virtual assistant. Seemed pretty straight forward to me, but it wasn't to those I needed to understand it—potential clients. It was almost as if everything I had done to be successful as an EA was actually holding me back as a VA. How was this possible? How could I change what I had trained to do for so many years? Who doesn't want a great executive assistant? Don't they know we're worth our weight in gold? The answer I got was a big fat "NO!"

Very few people you'll meet truly know and understand what an EA does. Think about it. How often do people think all you do is schedule calendar appointments, make travel arrangements, and take minutes at meetings? If only, right? Telling someone you're the "Jack or Jill of all things" still doesn't help your cause because no one realizes what the "things" are unless they already have an EA. And if they have one, they don't need you.

When I started my VA business, I made the decision to hire a business coach. It was one of the best things I could have done as I entered the new world of virtual assistance. As I began working with my coach, she talked about niching down. What? You want me to do less and ask for more money? Turns out she was right.

Executive assistants and virtual assistants are not and cannot be the same. What made you great in the office is exactly what will hold you back in the virtual world. Make no mistake, everything you know will provide great value to your VA business. However, you'll provide the most value to yourself.

Some of the fundamental differences between executive assistants and virtual assistants are:

- EAs support one person or one company with one mission. VAs support multiple clients, all with different missions and objectives.

- EAs are best when they can be all things to all people. VAs are best when they are specialized and serve as an expert to a select subset of people.

- EAs are paid based on their time. VAs are paid solely on their work. (It doesn't matter if it takes you five minutes or five hours.)

- EAs are employees. VAs are business owners, entrepreneurs, and CEOs.

Each VA is unique in his or her own way, just as each EA is unique. However, these four fundamental differences can hold back even the most seasoned executive assistant from true success as a virtual assistant.

The heart of a VA remains the same as an EA. We are cut from the same cloth and have the same service-minded blood coursing through our veins. A true virtual assistant runs a business to serve, to do the right thing, to know when to break his or her own rules and go beyond the extra mile or to run ahead by five. All of us support those we are working for and with. We perform our work with the same intensity as if our own name was on the front door.

Proud to Be a Virtual Assistant and Why It Matters

Virtual assistance describes how we do things (virtually), not what we do. This is why some VAs change their title. Even I, at one point, thought it might be a good idea to no longer call myself a virtual assistant. However, changing our title would also change why and how we provide the service, and that detail is too important to leave out.

In this age of remote working, people have come up with many different titles to describe to others what they do. You may be familiar with Online Entrepreneur, Digital Nomad, Freelancer, and others. None of those titles resonates with me, although I easily could put myself into any one of those categories. I still choose to call myself a virtual assistant because that is what I do. Let me share with you why it matters.

I am first and foremost an assistant who *serves* my clients. Service is at the heart of what I do. It takes absolutely nothing away from who I am as a business owner and entrepreneur. Those who have never been an assistant tend to take great offense at being called an assistant because they feel the term is beneath them. If you are an assistant, it is a term of great pride knowing how you make a difference to those you help.

As an assistant, your goal is to help whomever you're working for reach their dreams and vision. You take it on as a personal mantra. You are inspired by another person's divine leadership and are willing to go into battle with them because you believe so deeply in their cause. Yet, you choose to do your work behind the scenes. For the love of it. Not the fame.

Speaking with current and potential clients lights a fire in me. If it doesn't, then I know that person is not the right fit and I move on because I'm not the person who is going to help them get to the next level. That's the great part of being a business owner. You get to choose who you work with. However, those clients whom I do connect with have inspired me to do my greatest work. They are excited to discover a virtual assistant who created her business to work with someone just like them.

Today's world of virtual assistance combines service, knowledge, and expertise with partnership and collaboration. It's more than outsourcing tasks and to-do lists. The right VA is an extension of the client's business, provides client-facing work, and creates calm. The right VA takes ideas and turns them into realities. We don't offer the world yet another consultant— we offer our clients assistance in the areas they need it the most. We do the work.

Want to Know What Clients Really Want? Soft Skills and Professionalism.

I spend a lot of time connecting with virtual assistants and people who want to become virtual assistants. I can tell you there is only one thing I really care about when we have that first call—soft skills. Why? It's what the client really wants. On a personal and professional level, I'm on a mission to weed out VAs without soft skills because they make it hard on the rest of us.

Soft skills are character traits, social skills, attitude, and communication skills that help people perform their jobs well and succeed in their careers. When I tell you soft skills are important, I'm speaking the truth. When I tell you soft skills set you apart from the competition, I'm being serious. You can always improve on or learn new skills related to your work, but soft skills can't be easily taught.

The administrative profession has made great strides over the years. As we enter with force into the new era of virtual assistants, I'm constantly reminding clients not all virtual assistants are created equal. My goal is to promote the field of virtual assistance and all administrative professionals. Professionalism and soft skills go hand in hand.

Being a virtual assistant also doesn't exclude you from being professional. Many times when I speak with admins who are wondering if they should enter the virtual assistance profession, they express their concern about the number of virtual assistants already in the workforce. I assure them it's all about quality, not quantity.

We owe a level of professionalism to our clients. Depending on the type of clients and client communication tactics you have, this professionalism can vary. It doesn't go away. Professionalism not only shows respect for your clients, it also allows you to charge more money. That's right! Your attitude and demeanor are subtle in demanding it, but it makes the client feel confident in paying a higher rate.

You can be yourself *and* be professional. I'm professional but not always formal. You won't catch me wearing slacks or heels at home. I save that formality for when I meet with clients and potential clients in person. They are very likely to dress the same.

If your clients are yogis, then it probably is professional for you to wear yoga pants when having face-to-face meetings with them. What isn't professional is missing a phone call or appointment because you needed an extra Zen moment. If your clients are working mothers and you are one too, there are a lot of things you both can relate to, but it doesn't excuse you from missing deadlines or being late for appointments because the kids are sick or a practice runs late.

Let's not forget first impressions—they matter! I've interviewed many VAs via phone and online chat and have been extremely disappointed in their level of professionalism. Gum smacking, talking while driving, being constantly interrupted, and not having a good internet connection are extremely unprofessional. This is not what I would expect or allow during an in-person interview. I don't allow it virtually either.

You don't have to agree with or even like this, but it doesn't make it less true. Being a virtual assistant doesn't exclude you from being professional. You owe it to yourself, your clients, and your profession to set a good example. Plus, you reap the benefits!

How to Climb a Mountain in Business

> *"The journey of a thousand miles begins with one step."*
>
> —*Lao Tzu*

In June 2017, I went on a two-day hike along the Polish-Czech Friendship Trail, which runs along the border between the Czech Republic and Poland. It was exactly what I was looking for. Time to get away, clear my head, and exercise. What I gained was far greater.

I shouldn't have been surprised. When taken out of our everyday routines and put into new situations, our minds stop working on autopilot and start searching for patterns, things it can make sense of. We are forced to think more creatively.

Traveling the world, I became accustomed to many things I once thought different, strange, and even abnormal. My new normal became packing up my life every month and heading to a different country. I tried to learn new words, eat new foods, find my way around and inevitably I got very lost. Every month I was faced with daily living challenges as simple as finding the grocery store. However, several months into my global travels, I no longer thought of it as challenging. Simply a part of my life.

Hiking is something I enjoy very much. It's not something I regularly do, so my brain was working creative overtime. As we climbed the mountains along the Friendship Trail, I began to see how the same fundamental principles applied in business. I've broken down these fundamental stages in business into eight steps. There is also a bonus section included along with the complimentary workbook. To make the journey more enjoyable and beneficial, you must enter into a certain frame of mind as you begin to take your first steps.

Know your mile markers and when to follow new ones.

There were several different color trails we could have taken on our hike along the Friendship Trail. Not only was finding our mile markers necessary so we didn't get lost, they also served as a point of reference when it was time to depart from the path we were on.

Think about some mile markers you can create for yourself, reminders you're on the right track. You'll also want to create markers to let you know when to start down a new path. These could be at specific celebrations, the number of clients you are serving, the number of virtual assistants in your network, or when something is not going in your favor. It is crucial to know when the path you're on no longer will take you where you want to go.

Take small steps when you don't know where you're going.

As we trekked up the mountain, visibility levels dropped. Instead of being afraid, we took small steps and continued along our journey. Thanks to our mile markers, we knew we were on the right path. We just couldn't see far down that path.

Business can be scary when you can't see into the future. Even when you know you're on the right path, you still want answers and some kind of guarantee. Neither business nor life is designed that way. It's not always about making great leaps. Plan to take the small steps needed to advance, and you will get to where you want to go.

Plan to rest.

We had not just one but two options for places to sleep the first night. Bound and determined to succeed on this hiking trip, the certainty of cold and rain did not deter us. We had a plan. When we got to the first resting place for the night, we talked as a group to determine if we felt good enough to go the rest of the way. Knowing we still had daylight ahead of us and calculating the pace, we agreed it was safe to keep going.

As business owners, one of the things we forget to do is rest. I'm a huge offender. I'm great at planning vacations! However, when it comes to daily rest, my instinct is often to "power through" and get things done. This should be the exception and not the rule. Making plans to rest keeps you in top physical and emotional shape. Plain and simple, you can't make good critical decisions for your business when you're always running on empty. The last thing you want to do is get caught in a storm.

It can be a blessing to not see what's in front of you.

During the hike, there were several times we experienced a complete whiteout. At one point on the trail, there was a small fence of sorts, a chain signaling not to go beyond that point. As we walked a bit further, it became painfully obvious. We had been hiking near a cliff! Even though we couldn't immediately see it due to the whiteout, the cliff was there. Suddenly I felt a bit of fear and anxiety, an increased level of cautiousness I hadn't felt before.

There wasn't a need for me to be more careful. It wasn't even possible. Instinctively when I saw the fence, I moved to the opposite side of the trail. I was reminded that a lot of people aren't scared of heights until they look down. Having blinders on in business can be good. Keep your head up and look forward. When you can't see too far in front of you, consider it a blessing. No need to play the "what if" game. Don't be afraid of what you can't see and don't assume it's all bad.

You're always closer than you think.

When we were hiking, I pointed to a house off in the distance on top of a big mountain. People looked like ants going up and down the mountain. As I turned to my hiking partners to point it out (as if they didn't see it already), one of them said, "That's where we're headed." I laughed. I thought he was joking. In my mind, it would take forever to get there. Before I knew it, we were at the house looking down at where we were just hiking.

What you're working toward may seem far, far away. When you keep putting one foot in front of the other, you will get there. It's not as far away as it seems.

Stop to capture and celebrate the moment.

I'm terrible at remembering to take photos. My hiking partners often stopped me and said, "Melissa, take a picture." I was about to walk by an amazing view without realizing how far we had come and without celebrating the beauty of where we were. Sure, it wasn't the final destination. However, these are the opportunities to find joy in the journey.

Capture each moment of building your business. Journal. Keep track of where you are, where you've been, and where you're going. Truly celebrate all you've accomplished and how far you have come. Don't wait until you reach the top of your mountain. Find the joy in your business journey. I've created this workbook to help you along the way.

The journey is better when shared.

Without a doubt, this hike would not have been the same without my partners. The cold, the rain, the wind all made it very uncomfortable at times. Our creepy little hotel that reminded me of *The Shining* would have been awful without them. There would not have been laughter over meals. No one would have been there to help me help myself. It's called the Friendship Trail for good reason. The happiest people on the trail were those who weren't alone. We were able to pool our resources and strengths together. We physically and mentally lightened the load for one another.

No matter what type of virtual assistant business you have, you weren't meant to go at it alone. Whether you hire a coach, join an online group, or form a mastermind, share your journey with others. It will make the bad times seem not so bad, and they'll go by quicker. The great times will be celebrated by those invested in you and by those who want nothing more than for you to reach your dreams.

I choose not to do life or business alone. Sure, I could have traveled the world on my own. But why? Our little hiking group created better memories and left little to chance. My business is far too important for me to go at it alone and make costly mistakes along the way. I share it with a business coach, a mastermind group, colleagues, family, and friends.

In business, we all have mountains to climb and obstacles to overcome. Now that we've covered the basics, let's go deeper. It's time to prepare you for your own journey! Make sure you have completed the preliminary steps and download the workbook to get the most out of this book.

CHAPTER 1

Step 1: Creating Your Ideal Client Avatar (and Knowing How to Use It!)

What is an avatar? In the simplest terms, it is the most accurate picture of your *ideal* client—key word, "ideal." The biggest hurdle in getting your first client isn't that you're not targeting enough people, it's that you are targeting too many. When I ask VAs or aspiring VAs who their ideal client is, most don't have one. Or their term is very general. Your avatar should be so specific you could name the person and recognize them walking down the street. It's like your inner circle. A secret club.

When you have an ideal client and can easily describe not only what they do, what they need, and how you can support them, it paints the same picture in someone else's mind. Now each time someone meets your ideal client, they'll immediately let you know or refer you to that person. That's the power of having an ideal client.

Another reason to create your ideal client avatar is because it answers the most asked question among VAs—"Where do I find my clients?" Now you'll know where to find them. Once you know who the person is, you'll know where they hang out in person and online. Are they on Facebook, LinkedIn, Pinterest, Twitter? Are they part of private forums or groups? Will you have to go offline and meet people in person? Finding clients is as simple as going to where they are.

Beginning by creating the list of services you'll offer is the tail wagging the dog. The process of choosing your services first is just plain backwards.

Whoever is going to be paying you has to have a say in the matter. Let's not forget that one of the most commonly asked questions among VAs—only second to "Where do I find clients?"—is "How do I get rid of this client?"

Many virtual assistants will start with the services they *think* are in demand, the tasks they love to do, and the work that seems interesting. None of those are bad things. They are simply a bad place to start. I was no different. I tried to take what I *thought* was a valuable service and then find the clients who needed them. The problem is everyone could use your services, but not everyone will value you nor pay you what you're worth. Could you work for anyone? Yes. But you won't want to. Think of it like this—if you were searching for a job, would you apply for every position because you could perform the work, even if you didn't care for the company, the pay wasn't good, and there were no benefits? I certainly hope your answer is "No." The same applies to finding the ideal client for your VA business.

The thought of having a single ideal client when you could have many clients might seem like you're limiting yourself. I promise you that not having any clients at all or having the wrong clients is worse. We are looking for your sweet spot, the area where your clients and your services meet and you are earning money. Whenever there is confusion in your business about what to offer, who is buying, how to package services, you need to follow the money trail—a trail you can follow only if you know who your ideal client is. This is where I'll guide you through the questions you need to ask of your clients and yourself. Since this is your business, it all starts with you.

How Do You See Yourself as a Virtual Assistant?

*"We don't see the world as it is;
we see it as we are."*

—Anaïs Nin

As a virtual assistant matchmaker and consultant, I talk and write a lot about finding and working with your ideal client. However, it is just as important to know who *you* are. You are your first ideal client because you will naturally gravitate toward others like you. How you view yourself as a virtual assistant and a business owner will have a direct impact on the type of client you attract. There are many questions that must be answered by your ideal client. Before your client can answer these questions, you need to be very honest with yourself and know from the beginning who you are. No one will ever believe in you more than you believe in yourself and your business. When you begin to create your ideal client avatar, you also should ask the same questions of yourself.

Many virtual assistants don't realize their avatars closely mirror themselves. If your ideal client is a far cry from who you are, you may want to ask yourself what you have in common. This isn't a question of diversity. This determines the bond and values you'll share, the power of association and communication, and if this is even someone you want to work with. If this isn't someone you want to work with, you'll have to begin answering the questions again.

You don't have to know which services you'll offer to determine your ideal client. In fact, you won't know what is valuable to your ideal client until you know who they are. A long list of services your client *could* benefit from doesn't help. You're searching for the thing they feel is out of reach until you come along and provide assistance.

I consider myself a frugal person. There are things I refuse to pay $20 for. Could I use it? Sure. Does it promise to make my life better? Sometimes. Am I going to pay for it? Eh, who knows? My favorite purchases aren't things I need—they are things I want. Your ideal client should *want* and be excited to pay you. That's the difference between a client and an ideal client.

Below is a list of questions to get you started on the path to creating your avatar. These also can be found in your complimentary workbook. Your ideal client will have more specific questions for you to answer. However, you must know who the person is first.

- What are your ideal client's top three personal interests?

- What are your ideal client's top three business interests?

- What are your ideal client's top three recreational interests?

- What are your ideal client's daily activities?

- What are your ideal client's hobbies?

- What makes your ideal client happy?

- What makes your ideal client sad?

- What makes your ideal client angry?

- What is one thing your ideal client would like to add to their life?

- What is one thing your ideal client would like to remove from their life?

- What is your ideal client's daily commute?

- What are your ideal client's attitudes on religion?

- What are your ideal client's attitudes on politics?

- What media does your ideal client consume?

- Where does your ideal client shop?

- How does your ideal client dress?

- What vehicles does your ideal client own?

- What keeps your ideal client awake at night?

- What gets your ideal client out of bed in the morning?

- Who does your ideal client admire?

- What drives your ideal client crazy?

- To what does your ideal client aspire?

- What line of business is your ideal client in?

- What associations is your ideal client a part of?

- Where does your ideal client network?

- Which social media platforms does your ideal client visit most often?

- What is your ideal client's preferred method of communication?

- What is your ideal client's age?

- Name your ideal client:

- Find a photo of your ideal client:

Answer these questions to the best of your ability. Every answer is a key that unlocks a door about your ideal client. For instance, if your client doesn't own a vehicle, this provides insight about what kind of person he or she is—your client lives in a large city where a vehicle isn't necessary or he or she has chosen not to own vehicles to reduce their carbon footprint. This is very important information to have about your client. You might also share the same qualities. Don't overlook this. What is common for you is not common for everyone.

Don't simply answer the questions without thinking about how to use this information to your advantage. If you know your ideal client is on Facebook, where should you spend your time online? Based on your answers to these questions, create a day in the life of your client and figure out where you have to go to meet your client and his or her needs. This is a simple step that is most often missed after an avatar is created.

After answering the questions for your client, it's time to answer them for yourself. Imagine your future business self and where you want to be. Remember this is your business. You need clients to stay in business. However, you want the right clients so you *enjoy* being in business. Knowing what type of business you want will help shape the ideal clients you want to attract to your business.

Think about what you really want out of being a business owner. How many hours a week do you want to work? If you said 40, I can promise you that you'll struggle to get there and then when you do, you'll end up working more like 60 hours, including nights and weekends. In fairness, it was almost a trick question. You shouldn't think of your time in hours, rather in projects because that is how you will price your services. (I'll discuss pricing in chapter 3.) It also keeps you in an employee mindset, which can be hard to unravel after working as an employee for many years.

Begin to think of yourself as your own client avatar. (Don't skip this step!) If you had an assistant working for you, what would he or she be doing? What type of hours would you keep? What work would take up the majority of your time? Where do you work? Imagine a day in the life of your perfect life.

Imagining your perfect day now will help you shape it in the future. We'll discuss more about this when growing your business in chapter 7. However, if you start here, you won't have to do a "client cleanse" later. Right now you're thinking about getting your first client. Because I know you don't need to worry about this when you follow the steps I'll lay out for you, I'm focusing you on getting a full business without the unnecessary growing pains. This is how you do it.

Now using both your avatar and your ideal client's avatar, think about how you would answer the following questions so it is a win-win for your business and your client's:

- What things does your client want to experience?

- Does your client want to get ahold of you during specific business hours?

- Does your client care when you're online?

- How will the services you offer match the time you'll spend completing the services and the time you'll communicate with your client?

These should be a seamless transaction. You're not working around client demands. Your client's needs fit into your daily routine and aren't a distraction or a burden. They are cause for excitement and the challenging experience you crave.

Now that you've found the similarities, backgrounds, and values between you and your ideal client, ask yourself if you are leveling up. Your client shouldn't be at the same stage of business as you. If so, they won't be able to afford you. Your clients should be at least one stage up from you in business. This is how you earn more and provide more value. An added benefit is you can see how your client arrived at the next level and take those steps yourself. Your ideal client will unknowingly be a mentor for you.

From time to time when I go through this exercise with VAs, they create a fabulous ideal client avatar. Then when I ask what it is they have in common with this person, they can't say. More often, they won't say. It's okay for your ideal client to be someone you aspire to be like. Think about it—why would you want to work for someone you don't want to be like? Don't confuse not being at the same level as your client with not arriving yet. You have to believe you can and will arrive to what you aspire. Success is not a destination rather a frame of mind.

At the very last job I held before starting my VA business, I was the executive assistant to the assistant head of a school. This was just one of her many roles in life. She was also head of the English department, a teacher, a wife, a mother, a mentor, a speaker, a consultant, and an advocate for women in leadership. I didn't know it at the time, but she was my ideal client.

I learned from my male bosses certainly; however, there was only so much we had in common. Looking back, the best roles—both personally and professionally—I had were working for women just like her. All of them possessed many of the same qualities, and if I were to line them all up and begin to list the things they had in common, I could write another book. All were instrumental in my career and certainly led me to where I am today. They were also a perfect example of how I leveled up.

Over the next year, I watched my boss closely. How was she doing so much? How did she seem to have it all together, all the time? Why was she such a trusted confidant to so many? I took it all in. Even today I think back to her presentations and articles and read her favorite books. My clients now fill the same space for me.

You may be nervous when you level up while creating your ideal client avatar because this may be a completely different experience for you. It's normal. If you experience a little bit of fear, it comes with the territory. You've done this as an employee. Now experience this as a business owner. I promise you the satisfaction will be greater.

Once when I was consulting with a VA, she returned the form with a lot of comments written in. She had written things like, "I don't really do that" or "I think this question is irrelevant." If you feel it's irrelevant, chances are your client will feel the same way. If not, it's not likely you both are a good fit. This is why you create an avatar. You do it first to look at yourself and then second to identify the client, who that client is, and how you can associate to him or her. And, yes, even if the client is not the same sex, you can find many ways to associate.

The power of association is strong. While traveling, you'd be surprised what you notice and what you don't. When I arrived in new locations, sometimes I felt at home right away because there was something I could associate with—a coffee shop, a sign in English, music. In other countries, I felt as foreign as I was. Everything seemed backwards. The more out of place I felt, the more excited I became when I saw something familiar. On the days when it seemed everything was going wrong, seeing something I could associate with brought me comfort in a way nothing else could. Never underestimate the power to associate with your potential clients, especially when they need it the most.

Will you have clients who don't fit your avatar to a T? Sure. The difference is they seek you out, not the other way around. Your time and energy is best spent on the right clients, not the exceptions to your avatar. Think of it like this—if you were throwing a party, you could pick up everything you need from several different specialty stores and run yourself ragged all over town. Wouldn't you rather go to one location, a one-stop shop? In the beginning, don't waste time getting single clients the hard way. Clients similar to one another hang out at the same places.

Do You Know What Your Deal Breakers Are? They Matter.

One of the most powerful lessons I learned in my virtual assistant business came from knowing what my deal breakers are. Even more importantly *who* my deal breakers are. Too bad I didn't start with this.

It all started as I was writing the dreaded, but mandatory business plan. I was getting some assistance as to how to write my plans not only my thoughts out. Which means you'll have hard answers to seemingly easy questions.

When you start a business, there is no shortage of advice. People tell you where to find your clients, what groups to join, how to network, how to market, how to build your website, etc. What they don't commonly tell you is to know your deal breakers. If I would have started with this during the avatar process, I would have saved a lot of time, money, and frustration.

What is a deal breaker? It's anything in business that is a factor or issue that, if unresolved during negotiations, would cause one party to withdraw from a deal. In even simpler terms, think of it like dating. Are you willing to date a smoker? If the answer is no, that's a deal breaker.

Be just as clear on the type of clients you want to work with and those you do not. If you are not very clear and haven't drawn your own line in the sand, you are destined for trouble. You might as well plan on it because you haven't planned otherwise.

It starts when you go against your gut. You tell yourself lies like, "It won't be so bad." "I'll use that as vacation money." "This client could lead to the client I really want." The list goes on. Ultimately, we end up regretting that we accepted that situation because it was, in fact, a deal breaker.

Maybe you listened to a trusted friend or colleague. It may not be a deal breaker for somebody else, but it is for you and that's what matters. From the very start, you know you're in a bad place. Immediately when that person's email comes through or you see his or her name on your phone, you cringe. You can feel the life being sucked out of you for the tiniest things. This client or their work is a deal breaker for you. Plain and simple.

Pia Silva is a leading expert on niching and building brands. In one of her Forbes articles, "When We Started Turning Away Clients Our Business Really Took Off," she explains the power of saying no. She explains how not all dollars are created equal and that saying yes is actually killing your business—another counterintuitive principle that most people don't know or refuse to accept.

Not everyone is a good match for a virtual assistant, and they are surprised to hear such a thing coming from me, knowing I'm losing out on their dollars because of it. However, taking on a client who has unrealistic expectations is detrimental to my business and my mindset. Consulting a VA who is not bound and determined to put in the work isn't only a waste of my time, it's damaging to my reputation.

Some other deal breakers I have is when clients don't value my time or expertise. A no-show on calls, late to meetings, a last minute text that they can't make it. All those things are deal breakers. Having me jump through hoops is also a deal breaker. They are trying to put me through "tests" when they're expecting me to fail. Someone who doesn't want to set you up for success is someone who doesn't want to see you succeed. Why would you want to work for someone like that? Why would you want to work for someone you're never going to please?

Now let's talk about the clients we love. They ask for sample work and are willing to pay for your time because they believe you're worth it. They want to see you succeed. These are the ones we're willing to go the extra mile for, to take their late call, to answer their early email. We don't have to jump through hoops for them. We are looking to please them and get the work done at all costs. There is almost nothing we wouldn't do for them. And it's never a burden. Rather it's our pleasure.

Let's face it, the work is going to be challenging on its own. Life will bring you enough ups and downs, twists and turns. Murphy (as in Murphy's Law) will turn up left and right. These things we know. Don't invite more trouble into your business in the form of deal breakers.

Additionally, working with deal breakers will affect your other clients. That's not fair to them! It's like going into the office while you're sick. No one appreciates your working at half the pace and infecting them at the same time. Keep your germs to yourself!

Deal breakers come in all forms, in many shapes and sizes. Start asking yourself the hard questions and make a list. Then stick to it! You are a business owner now. Not only are you responsible for earning your money, you're responsible for treating yourself well as the most important person in your company.

Ideal clients are necessary. Is it possible to have more than one ideal client? Yes, absolutely. However, you need to focus on just one in the beginning to make sure this is in fact your target audience, or you could end up misleading yourself. I'll discuss more about having multiple ideal clients and how to package your services in chapters 3 and 7.

Summary

- Now you know the questions to ask to create your ideal client avatar. Not everyone is your ideal client. While you could work for anyone, you won't want to nor will all clients value you.

- You know how to use your knowledge of your ideal client to gain clients. Knowing what is important to your future clients, how you can associate with them, and what you already have in common will position you to work with those you were meant to work with.

- You've discovered what your deal breakers are and how they will damage your business. Knowing who your deal breakers are is instrumental and will help you to avoid many pitfalls. It will also help you get into the proper frame of mind of a business owner.

With the knowledge of who your ideal client is, how to gain them, and the deals you won't break in business, we can move on to chapter 2: Finding Your Niche and Monetizing.

CHAPTER 2

Step 2: Finding Your Niche and Monetizing

I've grown my business in several areas, but I wouldn't still be in business if I didn't niche when I first started. All the opportunities I've had resulted from the first opportunity to make money in my niche. Before that, my clients were piecemeal and I went through feast and famine cycles. Now my niche is education, something too broad to have begun with. Being broad is being bland, and I love what Pia Silva says about being bland—"Bland is not a flavor."

One of my least favorite sayings is "fail fast." For years I didn't understand the idea behind it. Why would anyone want to fail? Is it really necessary to fail? I was not a good student and the verbiage took me right back to school. I hated it. Failing, to me, was basically the worst thing in the world. Then I read a book called *Creativity Inc.,* written by Ed Catmull, the president of Pixar. He described failing fast in a completely new way which actually made sense to me—The idea of failing fast is so that you don't become married to it.

This is really great advice because not all of your niching ideas will work. Not all of my ideas worked, and some still don't. Not everything worked out the way I planned. But the longer I held on to my ideas before I tried to learn if they would work, the more married I became to them. The consequence was that it hurt more when the ideas didn't work. If your idea does work, you'll kick yourself for not trying it sooner. If it doesn't work, it doesn't hurt as badly and it's much easier to shake it off. All that time, effort, and energy can take a lot out of you.

Don't confuse quitting the services you offer with quitting your business. You're heading down a new, unmarked path. Don't be afraid to get off the current trail or stop to regroup and assess the situation. This is actually a best practice. As long as you're in business, you'll always be tweaking your model, brand, and services. What works today might not work tomorrow. Your clients may be the same, their needs may change, you may change, your desires may change. Everything is constantly evolving. Stay present in your business.

Fun fact: Did you know that Pixar's widely famous movie *Inside Out* was once a failed idea? It's true!

As you begin thinking about choosing your niche, consider talking to people about your ideas. A common thing I hear is, "I wanted to do XYZ, but I was told it's not scalable." In the beginning, don't worry about being scalable. Your first order of business as a business owner is to make money. You can find a way to scale later. Right now scaling is the least of your worries. Grow first, scale later. If you're not even close to client capacity, having a solid income coming in every month, and identifying your ideal client, there is nothing to scale.

Once you figure out how the money's coming in, you also need to have a system to replicate. Whether you want to change your ideal client, change your services, or business model, it all starts from figuring out where the money is coming in—your ideal client and ideal services will lead you to your niche.

Do the One Thing That Matters Most

You could have an excellent business full of value, but to the wrong person it makes no sense. Instead of selling umbrellas to those caught in the rain while wearing their brand-new suede shoes, you're trying to sell discounted umbrellas to people on a Sunday stroll in the park. It really comes down to not only bringing in more clients but being able to make better decisions about who your clients are and how they serve as a win-win for both your business and theirs.

As service providers, finding our area of focus is often called niching. Do you have to niche to become successful? No, not necessarily. Is it the fastest way to make money and get clients? Yes, absolutely. So many struggling virtual assistants have told me that besides not having an ideal client, their biggest problem is they don't know which service matters most to their clients. The process seems counterintuitive to them. Yet if you want more clients and to make more money, this is how you do it.

Keep in mind that VA businesses are no different from other businesses when it comes to building a successful business model. Nordstrom started as a shoe store. Amazon started as on online bookstore. Google started as a search engine. Where you begin is the start; it's not the end. Your goal is to learn how to make money every single month.

Why is this so important? Because if you are stressed over a lack of money, you cannot think clearly and you will no doubt miss out on opportunities right before your eyes. Why can it feel so hard? Because the process is not linear. You won't find the answers on an organizational chart.

When I arrived in Thailand in October 2017, it was after many hours of traveling, delayed flights, rescheduled flights, lost luggage, lack of sleep, and a lot of frustration. I wasn't able to take a hot shower for the first three days. Plus, I immediately began working graveyard shift hours. You could definitely say there were a lot of stressful things happening all at once.

The first days after my arrival, I went out in the late evenings in search of food and coffee. I found nothing satisfying and ended up eating awful instant soup cups from 7-Eleven. I walked what seemed like forever at 1 o'clock in the morning to a 24-hour coffee shop for my first cup of hot coffee. While I was full and caffeinated, I was not at all satisfied. I would have paid just about any price for a decent meal.

On my third day, the hot water had finally been fixed and nothing felt as good as taking a hot shower. I went out during the day and suddenly my eyes were opened to everything around me. On those first nights, I had walked by no less than six coffee shops, and there were three 24-hour coffee places closer than the one I had gone to. Food was plentiful and the number of options was almost overwhelming. In my defense, one day many shops were closed due to a national holiday. However, I didn't even notice what I was passing by. I didn't see what was staring at me. I literally didn't see the restaurant signs. How could this be?

When we miss the fundamental basics of our life, our vision is clouded. As the saying goes, "Money isn't everything, but it's right up there with breathing." In this particular case, the hot shower I missed was my currency. Without it I didn't feel comfortable going out during the day. I didn't feel like myself. It was as if I was carrying around days of baggage and travel that a cold shower couldn't remove.

When you have money issues and worries, you can miss opportunities and signs right in front of you. We make our lives harder than they need to be, and the obvious goes unnoticed. My goal is to get you making money as quickly as possible. Niching and knowing how to monetize is the answer.

Are You Struggling to Figure Out Which VA Services to Offer?

One of the most common questions virtual assistants ask is "Which services should I offer?" It's hard to narrow down because chances are you have many skills that are desirable to potential clients. This is especially difficult if you come from an executive assistant background. You'd get fired for doing less, let alone doing just *one* thing, no matter how well you did it. Remember, EAs and VAs are not the same. They are like cousins. What worked for you as an executive assistant will work *against* you as a virtual assistant.

The more services you offer, the more likely you are to confuse your potential clients. Your clients have the same issues as you. They will get busy, stressed, pulled in many different directions. When they look over your long list of services, they won't be able to process the information and are very likely to miss the one thing you could do that would benefit them the most.

More importantly, if you offer too many services you will be pulled in different directions without mastering a certain field. It's no longer just about the work. You're also a business owner so you need to act like one. Mastering a specific field is how you become known, how you get referrals and gain more clients. When you are known in your area of expertise, you can learn to duplicate your systems, diversify the way you earn income, and charge higher rates because you know the return on your client's investment.

One of the most common reasons VAs don't want to niche is because they are afraid of becoming bored. When niching is done right, you won't have to worry about this. However, in the beginning it is easy to do it wrong because we think in terms of our duties, not our strengths. When you work in your strengths, you'll be using a lot of your talents and abilities. Don't worry about becoming bored. This isn't your business model forever. When the time is right, you can expand your services and clientele. Niching is for now, not forever.

If you can't monetize with one service, you can't do it with two, three, or four. When you offer that many to begin with you won't know what works and what doesn't. We all love what we do, but love doesn't put food on the table or keep a roof over our heads. My goal is to get you to your first client and then work on creating a thriving business. We'll spend more time in chapter 7 learning how to grow your business. That's where we get to create magic together, and it's my favorite part of consulting with VAs!

To find the right answers, you need to ask yourself the right questions. Here are five questions to ask yourself. Remember niching isn't only about the actual services you'll offer. It's also about the unique market you'll be serving.

- **What do you love AND what gives you energy?** You're going to be doing it for a living. Every. Single. Day. It's not only about loving the work. You should find energy from it as well. If not, even if you love what you do, you will get burned out very quickly.

- **What comes naturally to you?** When you think about this question, don't limit yourself to your business life. Think about your personal life as well. Don't dismiss something because it is easy for you. That is a huge mistake! What is easy for you is often very difficult for someone else.

- **What do you dislike?** Inspiration can come from need, but it can also come from frustration. Is there a product or service you want to offer because what is currently available is subpar? Do you think you can do something better or for a greater good? Is there no one addressing your specific needs? Remember you don't have to reinvent the wheel. Slight changes can cause huge shifts.

- **Are you part of a niche market already?** Oftentimes you may look outside yourself while the answer you're looking for, is in fact, you. What unique qualities do you possess? What groups are you a part of that you can tap into? Do others ask you questions about certain topics or markets because they consider you the expert? Use all these things to your advantage.

- **What do you believe in?** When you believe in something, you exude passion and excitement. It's undeniable to those around you and they want to jump on your train.

Are you beginning to see a non-linear path? Finding your niche isn't meant to be difficult, although it can feel that way! It is tapping into the person you already are, simply doing less and getting paid more! That is why it is so difficult. Our natural instinct is to be all things to all people, and that won't get you anywhere but frustrated and burned out.

The process of niching can seem difficult because you have to drill down and discover not only what you're good at, why you enjoy it, and who is going to pay for it, but then you have to learn how to explain it. Again, this is a process. It doesn't happen overnight. We frequently overlook our unique niches because we do these things naturally and without thinking. We take our skills for granted.

My own story took more than a year to be revealed. When I stumbled across it, all of a sudden it made perfect sense. I felt like I was searching to find the needle in a haystack. In the middle of a hayfield. While suffering from hay fever. With no medicine to cure me or at least to dull the agony.

On the other side of my story, it became painfully obvious to me. When people ask me about how I got started, the yearlong journey turned into a five-minute story that rolled off my tongue. Often VAs will tell me, "Wow, that's really great! You've done a lot!" Sure. Now. When I was going through the process, I wasn't able to see things as clearly. I was trying to follow an upward flow when it was the rabbit trails that did me the most good.

Working with my business coach, I had fought some fierce battles as she kept telling me to go deeper. I did everything on the surface. On the surface is where we get to *see* our work. We package it up all nice and pretty and have something to show for our efforts. Forget about yourself as a VA.

Think about yourself separate from your work. Seems counterintuitive, doesn't it? You're on the other side of the table now. This is how your clients think. They have to go through the same processes. Going through it yourself will benefit not only your business but theirs as well.

Now take the answers from those five questions you just answered and decide what you would like to be known for. Calling yourself a virtual assistant does not provide who you serve with *what* types of services you offer. It only tells people *how* you'll be serving them. So the real question becomes "What do you want to be known for?"

When thinking about your clients, remember they need and want specific things for their businesses. They're not comparing apples to apples or even apples to oranges when they're looking to hire a VA. No, they're choosing you from the entire fruit stand. What are you so known for that your potential clients know to choose you the moment they see you? Remember, they're busy and will gravitate toward the shiny object.

The virtual assistance world could be called a crowded market. However, when you know who is going to choose you and why, it begins to get less crowded. When you can nail down the experience, the crowd is gone. When you can shine, you get picked out of the crowd.

Complete this sentence: You are the VA who _____ (fill in the blank) for the client who_____ (fill in the blank). From here all your other questions will be answered, such as.

- Who needs it?

- Why do they need it?

- Who will value what you're known for?

- Who will pay for it?

You must be willing to get specific. Saying you want to be known for being the best VA in the world is pretty hard, especially since we don't have any type of competition to prove it. Being known for providing the best customer service is too vague because no one knows what that service is.

You may not know what you want to be known for yet. And that's okay. I didn't either. So start by listing everything you're good at. EVERYTHING. This will cause you to overlook the "whys" and "hows" of your career. Aim to make a list of 100 things. If you can think of more, keep going. What might seem insignificant can lead you to understanding yourself better and in a way you never considered before. I promise you'll discover a pattern. Then you'll figure out how to connect the dots to create the lifestyle you want. Suddenly you'll find yourself staring at things you've overlooked for years.

To get to this place even faster, enlist the help of everyone you know, everyone you've worked for. They don't even have to be your closest friends. In fact, someone you had a casual conversation with at soccer practice or at a volunteer event might have a first impression of you that's completely separate of your longtime friends who have watched you grow over the years.

To better understand how this process might look, let me share my story with you. I had positioned myself as an executive virtual assistant, but there was a major flaw in my plan. Most people don't know what that is or what that means. Promoting yourself as "saving time" (this is the biggest one among VAs, and I might have been the biggest offender) isn't specific enough. Everything and everyone claims to do this.

Partly on the right track, I sought out what made me happy and excited me—calendar management—but that turned out to be a superficial answer. I was competing against apps and other electronic tools, which I was happy to do. The clients who could have benefitted the most from what I was offering didn't hire me. What was worse, I couldn't even give my services away. It was a crushing blow.

So I drilled down to figure out why my calendar management skills are so useful—it's because I can make a person's life easier, filling in their business, personal, and family goals and commitments. I could forecast the future, plan for delays, and find others to take over when necessary to keep moving forward. Because I managed my supervisors' calendars successfully, they could begin projects they wanted to but never had the time for.

I realized that because I could manage calendars well, that made me a "productivity expert." This led me to remove "assistant" from my title. But being a productivity expert wasn't right because that meant I was trying to teach the wrong people to be productive. I don't believe my clients should be productive in the same manner that I was as an assistant.

At this point I hit a wall. How could I always get a 9 to 5 job and be in demand, but now I couldn't sell my services? I was frustrated, upset, discouraged, and wondering how long I could go on like this financially. How long could I stand being miserable without work? Then I got a message from a gentleman on LinkedIn. He wanted to speak to me about working together.

During our conversation he described to me all the things he needed, many of which I could not do. At the end of our conversation, I told him I was exactly who he was looking for, an executive virtual assistant who could manage the project of writing his first book. He jumped on the opportunity and suddenly I found my niche. I would be an EVA project manager for aspiring authors with full-time jobs. It made complete sense. I love books, and I could use my calendaring and productivity skills. I also loved the personal attention I could give to my clients by mapping out the process. Most of all, I enjoyed the challenge and the variety. I would simply find the right people to do the things I couldn't do.

After I discovered my niche, I began telling people what I did and what type of VA I was. Everyone got it. I received referrals, and more people requested consultations. Because it was a strong niche that played to my strengths, I could get better, faster, more efficient—take on multiple clients and yet keep it all very personal. I loved my work and my clients. Had I started with my personal strengths, gifts, passions, desires, and hobbies, I probably would have arrived at this point in my career much sooner.

Look at that list of 100 things you're good at doing. After you've asked friends and acquaintances to give you feedback, you should have uncovered some of your best qualities and abilities. Now you can begin to look at who your ideal clients are and determine what they are missing from their professional lives, the pains they feel that either keep them up at night or keep them working all the time.

Working backwards into my ideal client, I discovered that he was a male who had a career and wanted to write a business book. The problem was he could not find the time to write a book in the midst of his other work duties and life commitments. That's where I stepped in. My ideal client was searching for accountability—someone to research editors, book printers, Amazon setup, formatting, cover design, creating a timeline, and taking care of other tasks that may come up as he dealt with his daily work. This was my niche.

I found it because I found my ideal client. When I could see the similarities in all of my clients, both personally and professionally, I began to see what they wanted versus what they said they needed. How I sold it wasn't by saying what I did, it was by saying who I helped and the end outcome—I virtually assisted aspiring authors with full-time employment finally publish their books.

Niching doesn't have to be a specific skill or a single service, although it could be and that is often the case if you provide more technical services. Niching can be your client base and their needs as a whole. Remember when I said niching was for now, not forever? My business has grown, and I no longer serve clients in this capacity. In chapter 5, I'll share with you how this first niche led to where I am now.

There was something different about making money now versus when I was struggling. At first when I told people what I did for a living, some told me it was a great idea, said it was valuable, and assured me I was in demand. However, not one of them was forking over any cash. Fans are not clients. Don't confuse the two. When someone says you have a great idea but they aren't willing to pay for it, you have a problem. This is where VAs can often get stuck. Forget the compliments and go for the cash.

Monetizing

I thought I had an edge, a leg up because I cared about and loved what I do so deeply. "Do what you love and you'll never work a day in your life." A great quote with an untold great truth. Until you figure out how to make money, you've got an expensive, draining hobby. So, yeah, you won't be working.

My wake-up call about not making money came one day during a conversation with my brother. I was frustrated that I wasn't making enough money, and my brother told me about a guy he knew who was doing extremely well for himself. At first I was confused. I didn't know a person in his field could make so much. My brother explained it wasn't his day job that was providing all the extra cash. He was making this money on the side. What? It wasn't a get-rich-quick, online marketing, or turnkey business. This was an in-person service business he was running while keeping his full-time day job. He even had a few people working for him part-time.

As I pressed my brother for more information, I was getting angry, even jealous, which isn't an emotion I experience often. Why him? Why not me? I live and breathe what I do. This guy doesn't even like it. Even with all the money he's making, he had no desire to quit his day job because that is what he really loves. He's certainly not smarter than me. What bizarre world are we living in?

I made a comment about things being "fair" to my brother. Life wasn't fair because here I was doing the work I love and barely getting by, and then here's a guy who hates what he does on the side and he's making money hand over fist.

That's when it hit me.

This guy and I both saw a market need, so we had that in common. We both saw value in our businesses. Got it. When I first started, I got out of bed every morning to do the work I love for little to nothing. This guy wouldn't get out of bed for less than his premium price because he *didn't* love it. His price was fixed, non-negotiable. He knew the value and the service, the demand in the market, and had no fear of loss. That's where I was going at it all wrong.

After learning of this guy's story, I was bound and determined to make money. No longer was I going to let this guy, who has no idea who I am, beat me in business. Doing what you love doesn't mean you will make money. You have to make that decision on your own. Figure out a way to charge for everything you do. This doesn't mean you nickel and dime clients, nor does it mean you overcharge. However, when someone says, "I'd pay for XYZ," pay attention. Don't think it's ridiculous and don't say you'll do it for free because it will take you all of five minutes.

The hardest part of monetizing what you do isn't deciding on pricing, although we'll cover this in the next chapter. The hardest part is figuring out what you're monetizing because being good at something doesn't mean people will pay you for it.

Here's another tip—people won't always pay for what they need. Crazy but true. Value, ability, worth, outcome, and expectations—that is what you're monetizing. Notice I didn't list skills. Skills are important, but your client has skills as well. Chances are they've already done what they are willing to pay you to do. You will rarely wow anyone with your skills.

The way you will wow someone is by *how* you do things. The how is what you monetize. People used to tell me to "sell the sizzle not the steak." I knew what they were saying and yet I couldn't get it right. I was too focused on all the things I could do. All the things I have done. All the people I've helped in the past. In the simplest of terms, say who you help and how you do it. (I'll share some examples of this in chapter 5 when we cover the elevator pitch.)

Monetizing is making money, which means you have to ask for it. Unapologetically. Too many virtual assistants are afraid to ask for money. If you can't ask, no one is going to give it to you. All the clients, colleagues, and contacts I had who were making the kind of money I wanted to make had no problem asking for it unapologetically. Without batting an eyelash or stuttering. I'll share a secret with you—it's easier to ask for money when you know someone has it. So how do you know who has it? Follow the money trail toward your ideal client.

If you know what your ideal client needs, then you'll know how much they will pay for that service based on what they have paid for in the past. What do they charge their clients? This won't be exactly the same for all of your clients, but you will find strong similarities. Some of the things I need I actually enjoy doing. I need to do a lot of writing, but I'll never hire a ghostwriter. Not even if that person was a *New York Times* bestselling author. Other tasks that are simple, I'll happily throw money at someone to do them for me. Which problems do your clients throw money at? No matter how simple, easy, or remedial, figure out a way to charge for it.

To dive deeper into this subject, there is no better book I'd recommend than Dorie Clark's latest book, *Entrepreneurial You: Monetize Your Expertise, Create Multiple Income Streams, and Thrive.* Remember you're in business for the long haul. This is not a get rich quick book, and the strategies Dorie suggests will bring you long-term benefits.

Summary

- Now you know why you should really fail fast in business, so you don't become married to your ideas. It's perfectly normal if you don't end up with what you started with!

- You've learned the importance of niching and why it's for now, not forever. Remember, you don't want to be bland. "Bland is not a flavor."

- You know how offering more services in the beginning confuses your ideal client. Don't trust your clients to order á la carte from your service menu. Know how you want to stand out and what you want to be known for.

- Ask yourself the five questions to begin the process properly. If you want the right answers, ask yourself the right questions and don't skip the steps.

- You know why loving what you do too much is a bad thing. Love not only what you do but also yourself in the process. Know your value and your worth.

As we continue building your business, it's time to take care of the nuts and bolts, and that's what we'll be covering in the next chapter. This is the necessary preparation that must be done before you begin gaining clients.

CHAPTER 3

Step 3: The Nuts and Bolts of Your VA Business—Business Planning, Pricing, Sales, Negotiations, and Contracts

The next step to creating your VA business is writing a business plan. I remember dreading each business plan I ever made. They were exhausting, and I didn't know why I needed a plan. What I thought I needed was clients and money. Later I learned how much this would cost me. If you think about the things we plan—trips to the grocery store, weekly dinner menus, our next vacation—doesn't it make sense that you should give attention to the thing that pays for all the other things?

A business plan's primary purpose is to create the vision of your company on paper so you know what you're doing. This is your roadmap. From there you can plan all the other facets of your business, from sales and marketing to growth and design.

You've already done much of the hard work that goes into a business plan. You already know your audience, your niche, and your value. Now it's simply a matter of putting it on paper. What you need to add to your business plan now is how you'll run your company. What do you sell? What do you charge? What are your short-term and long-term goals?

The power of putting these things on paper is not only so it is clear, it's also to show inconsistencies. We don't mean to be inconsistent. Somehow it just happens. Have you ever had something so clear in your mind and then when you wrote it out, no one else understood? Maybe you didn't understand anymore either. That's because no one can write a business plan in their heads. Period.

Pricing

When it comes to setting fees, it's easy to make this an emotional decision—especially when you think of your bills and purchases in an emotional way. Your pricing and emotions actually have very little to do with one another. Nor can you base your pricing on how much money you made as an employee. The faster you get rid of the employee mindset, the better off you'll be.

I've read no better book on the subject than *Profit First* by Mike Michalowicz. If you are a Dave Ramsey follower, this book is Dave Ramsey approved. The book is so powerful that I send a signed hardcopy to all the VAs I consult with as well as my online class participants. I have a lot of favorite books, but this one is more than a favorite. It's a necessity, and I wish I had read it when I first started my business.

Along with all the practical applications, this book shows you how to set your prices, take the emotion out of paying bills, and think like a business owner and entrepreneur. Trust me when I tell you, you need to read this book.

How Do You Know if Your Pricing Is Valuable to Your Market?

Your pricing shouldn't be a struggle or a secret. Your goals should be to know how to price your services and then find the right client to not only pay those prices but also find you extremely valuable.

When I interview VAs, I'm always intrigued when someone is hesitant to share their prices. Knowing my client's budget, my job is to stay in the ballpark or be able to justify why going with the higher fee is worth it. Hesitancy makes me wonder if you're hiding something, making up prices as you go along or not confident in what you are charging. Often, it's the latter.

Usually it has less to do with the fees and more to do with a lack of confidence that the client can afford the fees. This tells me the virtual assistant hasn't done enough homework on who his or her client is and what that client finds valuable.

Virtual assistants can learn from big businesses. You may not be grossing millions or billions of dollars, but good business principles are something we all benefit from. At the end of the day, we're all trying to turn a profit, not break even or avoid going bankrupt.

In a First Round Review article, "It's Price Before Product. Period," Madhavan Ramanujam is the "Price Whisperer." Let's break down his advice so it can be applied and easily implemented into your VA business:

Client's Willingness To Pay (WTP)

You can't assume all people value you and your services in the same way. Furthermore, you can't expect someone to be willing to pay a higher rate simply because he or she can afford to. While you need to make money and monetize your services, stop offering more. Offer exactly what your potential clients want at the price they are willing to pay. If the ideal client avatar you created isn't putting money in your pocket, one of you has to change.

Feature Shock

This is one of the most common issues for virtual assistants, and it was the hardest for me to overcome when I first started as VA as well. Clients want the *one* thing. Think about your favorite products. They only do one thing. Even if you see that product as a multi-feature item, it isn't. The team that created that product was smart enough to make it feel like more to you, but the end result was one thing. Discover your clients' one desired result and create your services to meet that need.

Undead Ideas

I love this term because it's intriguing, much like the services you are offering. The problem is no one is willing to pay you for it. Like a zombie clinging to a life that is already dead and gone, you hold on to the belief that others just haven't caught on yet. For me, this was calendaring. Calendaring is my great love, passion, and pet peeve when done wrong. There are so many apps, articles, and "experts" on the subject that I was determined this was going to be my platform. I was fixated on finding the right client to pay me for my services. I had so many ideas surrounding it. None of them ever caught on, and if I never changed, I would have been out of business a long time ago. My business and service model was in the undead zone.

Pricing is personal but not emotional. It's personal to you based on how much you need and desire to live on. The client also has a very personal point of view. Hiring a virtual assistant is an added business expense until it becomes an investment. You don't have the luxury to get upset if someone says you're overpriced. Do your homework and price accordingly. Don't make the mistake of putting your product before pricing or your emotions before your personal needs.

One of the most common statements I hear from VAs is "I wouldn't even know what to charge for that." This is not meant to be a guessing game. By now you should have a good idea of what your client can afford, what he or she is willing to pay, what your value is, and what you need to make. Don't forget to read Mike Michalowicz's book *Profit First*! His method will help you with your personal budgeting and how to manage the cash flow for your business.

Based on your ideal client, determine if you are going to price yourself hourly, by the project, with a flat fee, or on a retainer basis. How do you know which is right for you? Look to your clients. How they charge for their own services is a major indicator for how they like to pay.

Tip: If you are in the first year of business or virtual assisting in addition to your full-time job, you should either be charging by the project or a flat fee, and you should not sign any contract for more than three months at a time. Here's why. During your first year, you'll be learning a lot. You may find you don't like the services you are offering as much as you thought you would. You are likely to find you need to raise your prices. It's very possible you'll grow quickly, and your ideal client avatar might change. Having clients that are short-term and pay per project will allow you to part ways naturally and raise your prices if needed in a way that serves you and the client, creating a win-win situation. Even if you find that you dislike the project you agreed to do, you'll see the light at the end of the tunnel and can easily see that project through to the end.

If you are working as a VA on the side, you should never charge by the hour. You are already working enough. You'll never get ahead by putting in more hours, nor will you figure out how to work less and make more money. Instead, you'll actually penalize yourself for getting faster and more efficient. Then you'll have to work twice as hard and find twice as many clients to bring in the income you need. You can't do this, in any business, if you are trading your time for money.

When I first started out, my pricing was based not on what I needed or desired; it was based on what other VAs, who I felt were similar to myself, were charging. Even still, it was hard for me to charge $30 an hour, something I find laughable now. Because I had not taken the proper steps to determine who my ideal client was and the value I brought to my clients, I was attracting clients who also didn't really know what they were doing and what value they needed. And ultimately those clients didn't have enough extra income to afford me. My mindset was in the wrong place.

How to Price Your Services

Thinking about your ideal client, consider the following:

Remember where you live is irrelevant to the client. It doesn't matter to your client if you live in an expensive area and need to charge more. Because your feature is that you can work from anywhere, it can't also be the reason why your prices are higher. The whole point of being virtual is so the client can get the best candidate from anywhere. If location becomes a factor, your client could easily find someone in another state or country with cheaper prices.

Consider the client's fee structure. If your clients charge by the hour, use this as your guide. How much do they charge? If they make $150 an hour consulting and your fee is $50 an hour, that's one-third of their revenue. Don't forget their other expenses as well. However, if you know that your potential clients are booked solid and you'll only be working five hours a week, then it becomes less of a factor. A client charging $100 an hour or less is not likely to hire you at $50 an hour because that's half of their income before taxes and expenses. Either you need to lower your rate or change the type of client you want to work with.

Additionally, consider how the client views your hourly rate. Are they used to paying top dollar? Are you positioned to command your hourly rate? No matter what you charge, you should be able to present your prices with confidence. If you aren't confident in your hourly rate, your prospective clients won't be either. Practice telling people how much you charge per hour until you can do it without wanting to immediately discount the rate in your mind.

Know the mindset of a client that charges by the project. If your ideal client offers packages based on projects, take this into consideration. The mindset of someone who charges flat fees is they don't like any surprises and appreciate all-inclusiveness. These types of clients are constantly concerned about hidden fees and bottom lines. They want to know everything they will get for their money, not everything you offer. This is the ceiling mindset.

For instance, when talking with two different VAs, one may offer an hourly rate and guestimate how much time it will take to complete a project. The other will offer a flat rate and *tell* the client everything included and how long it will take to complete. No client will ever think you're going to complete something in less time than you will. They're always worried it will take more time. If clients believe you should have completed a project in less time than you actually did, you still haven't won them over. Make sure you are targeting the right client with your pricing.

It is much more likely this type of client will go with the second VA because he or she gives the client peace of mind—the client knows the ceiling limit. With the hourly virtual assistant, the client will constantly be worried about how many hours could be racked up and how long the project will take. The added benefit is the second VA appears to be the clear expert because only someone who has done it many times can give you firm dates, deadlines, and prices.

Consider this. One car mechanic charges $75 an hour and tells you it will take about an hour and a half of labor to repair your car, but he admits he really won't know until he gets under the hood. Another mechanic says he could do the job for $150 out the door. Which one will you choose? I'd go with the latter mechanic because I know there won't be any surprises or unforeseen costs. (Can you guess how I charge *and* pay for services?)

Your clients' perception is their reality. Know how clients perceive your value. It's your job to constantly make the connection between you and them. They are not going to do it on their own. Force the client to see you as the expert and as a VA who offers value by pricing accordingly.

Packaging Your Services

How your clients view your pricing is based on their perceived value. What you consider to be the most valuable part of your service might be completely different than what they consider to be the most valuable. When you itemize your services, you run the risk of oversharing and being scrutinized in a manner you wouldn't be if you simply packaged your services together.

In the beginning you'll likely have only one package. That is fine. Whether you have one package or multiple packages, you are asking your clients to self-identify the package that's right for them based on their needs, not based on your price.

Far too often, packages are simply buy now or buy later. There is no win for the client. It is only a win for you because you get to charge more now rather than wait for payment later. However, when you know what your clients need at each stage of business, you show them what you're offering isn't just a package that costs more. It's a package that meets them where they are in their business. Furthermore, you shouldn't identify your pack-ages as "A, B, C" or "Gold, Silver, Bronze" because those are ambiguous terms for your clients.

Here are three ways you might package services targeted toward a business coach:

Package 1 = Starter Package

For the business coach who is just starting out. You have an email list of 500 names or less. You need to create systems and processes for your new email leads, a newsletter to stay in touch with your current email list, a lead magnet, a campaign, and a funnel system to track where you convert leads into sales. Price $$$$. Priced as a one-time fee with a monthly maintenance package or as a monthly fee based on creating new campaigns, newsletters, and growing the email list.

Package 2 = Growth Package

For the business coach who has a backlog of clients waiting to work with her. You have an email list of at least 1,000 names. You need to create more personal systems and processes for your current, past, and future clients. You want to establish an online community (or manage an existing one) for current and past coaching clients. You need website updates and maintenance, billing and invoicing, appointment scheduling, and monthly newsletter support. Price $$$$. Priced as a recurring flat fee. This client is too busy to take over anything you create. He or she needs you to do the dirty work. Additionally, you could provide add-ons in the form of social media management, but only if you know how to convert followers into clients. If not, don't offer it. Not coming through in that one area will affect how your other work is perceived.

Package 3 = Diversifying Your Income Streams

For the business coach who is looking to create online courses, prioritize speaking engagements, host boot camps or retreats, or write a book. You are ready to diversify your income streams through all or some of these ways. On top of the daily needs of email, invoicing, billing, and online community engagement, you need a VA to manage your projects and make sure nothing falls through the cracks. While your business continues to grow and you find yourself in demand, I will manage your current projects, forecast future needs, and be the go-to person for you, your clients, and those contacting you about speaking engagements and interviews. Price $$$$. Priced as a recurring flat fee. You will only be able to handle a few clients at this level so charge accordingly and appropriately.

Package 1 is your bread and butter. It is easily tailored to fit any coach, consultant, or the like who needs processes and systems put in place. The monthly maintenance is a great system to keep generating income and creates a win-win for the client. You should be able to duplicate the system and have a thriving business on this model alone.

Package 2 is the hardest package to sell. This client probably didn't hire anyone early on and has been doing all the work. It's much harder to pay someone else to do it now. Their mindset is a little harder to shift than someone who knew their investment paid off right from the beginning. You can plan to have more calls and follow-ups with this client than the others. It's hard to find clients for this "middle" package. Either they think it's still too early to need your services, or they feel they're at the tipping point and need help now before it's too late.

Package 3 is for your premium client, and this is easy to sell if you get the verbiage right for your ideal client. If you have a hard time selling this package, don't look to the price first. Instead, look at the verbiage. Most likely, a key ingredient is missing that lets the client know this package is the right one for them.

You'll easily be able to keep track of which package is selling and which isn't. If you offer a package and never sell it, get rid of it. As long as you hold on to that service, you'll never make room for new opportunities. If you constantly upsell a package, keep it. Don't get rid of what is working!

Here's another reason you want your clients to identify services for themselves—they're not necessarily going to identify VAs based on our selection of services. A long list of services offered by virtual assistants is meant to read like a menu. *Pick what you want and let me know how I can help*. The problem is your client doesn't know it's á la carte. Instead of selecting what they need, clients seem to focus on what they don't need and dismiss the rest of your services. Your clients aren't looking for something generic, they are looking for something specific. How do you overcome this? By speaking to your ideal client. A conversation between just the two of you. We'll cover this in the next chapter.

Listing prices on your website comes down to two things—do you want to have a conversation or not? I sell my services based on conversations, so I don't list my prices on my website. Potential clients want to speak with me, and I want to speak with them. My conversion rate is much higher after a consultation.

If you are not concerned about having conversations with clients and believe you have a click-to-buy business, then yes, list your prices on your website. Few VAs have this luxury in the beginning. I highly suggest not listing your prices and instead speak directly with your potential clients. What you gain from every conversation in the beginning is far more valuable than selling one service or package. If you do it right, you'll have succeeded in both.

Pricing Is Not a Competition

I never could have commanded my current income when I first started as a VA. I'm a very competitive person, so I found myself competing with other VAs who I thought were like me. This turned out to be a race to the bottom. Your competitors don't determine your pricing.

I remember the first time I ever charged to match a client with a VA. It was freeing in a way I didn't expect. For the first time, I had no idea what to charge because I didn't know anyone else who was providing this service. When he asked my price, I blurted out, "$599." Why? Because I had just received a bill for the same amount. Afterward I thought about how cheesy it sounded, and I promised myself I would never do that again.

With no known competition and no prices to copy, I finally started pricing my services the right way. I based my pricing on what my ideal client would *happily* pay, taking into consideration my time, efforts, lifestyle choices, and worst case scenario. When I got real about my time, my value, and how many clients I could serve at once, I finally was charging what I was worth. As I worked through the process, I began offering tiered services and packages for clients to self-identify. I worked through trial and error, and I followed the money trail. I was able to raise my prices quickly with both confidence and success.

One thing I knew for sure was I was going for quality not quantity. I was going to be Tiffany not Walmart, and that is the type of client I was going to attract as well. Sure, Walmart will serve far more clients, but it's because they have to. Plus, I'll give you a secret tip—the more services you offer, the more discounted prices your clients think you should offer. When you position yourself as a one-stop shop, people naturally want a discount. When you position yourself as a boutique, your clients will expect to pay more. Never forget that your price also dictates the service.

Jeffrey Shaw, author of *Lingo: Discover Your Ideal Customer's Secret Language and Make Your Business Irresistible*, started his career as a photographer before becoming a coach, podcast host, speaker, and author. When he transitioned into the luxury market, his competitors were not other photographers, they were painters. By positioning his pricing to create the perception that his photos were masterpieces with an exact likeness, he was able to capture the market. He recognized the value he was bringing to his clients, and he set his prices strategically, not emotionally.

As virtual assistants, we are at a great advantage. We can be very nimble. Offer new services as soon as they come up, change your price structure as needed, and create a new business model every month until you find one that works. Don't be discouraged. Be smart when it comes to pricing, and your clients will pay you for it.

Collecting Payments

To your clients, receiving bills at the end of the month is like getting a credit card bill after a big vacation. Your client just took the vacation of a lifetime and a month later when they open their credit card bill, they forgot the nice hotel where they stayed, the tasty meals, the amazing excursions, and the memorable souvenirs. All they see is the large total at the bottom of the bill. They can't even remember what the beach smells like anymore. This is how they feel when you send your bill at the end of the month.

On the reverse end of the spectrum, when your monthly fee is paid upfront, the client isn't worried about racking up hours or getting surprises at the end of the month. This is like resort pricing. It's all inclusive. Nothing to come back and haunt them later.

If you aren't going to get paid upfront, you need to set up weekly payments. This is for the benefit of both you and your client. If you provide technical and project support, the minimum amount to charge upfront is half. After that you can charge in project increments.

Another downside to hourly pricing is that the client will naturally scrutinize an itemized bill. That's what most of us do with an itemized bill. Do you ever look over the details of a bill with a flat rate? Probably not. As long as it's the same amount, you just keep paying. Your clients will do the same.

Sell is Not a Four-Letter Word

Oh, the dreaded "sell" word! Why don't we like sales? It probably has to do with the stereotypes that come along with the idea of selling. Think "used car salesman." We don't like when people offer us what we don't need.

News flash! This is your business. You get to run it any way you'd like! You don't have to be salesy or dishonest or anything else you don't like in a salesperson. Plus, because you know who you're selling to and the value you bring to them, you don't have to worry about coming across as pushy or obnoxious. You should see yourself as a gift to your ideal client because you're offering exactly what they are looking for.

If you're anything like I was when I first started out, I would have done anything not to have to sell. I used to think, "Wouldn't it just be easier if people simply knew to pay me?" I fought the idea of having to sell my services until one day it no longer felt as though I was selling. Instead I was now telling my potential clients how I could solve their problems.

Nothing is more powerful than your mindset when it comes to selling. With your ideal client avatar, you should know exactly who you are selling to and who you aren't. You can seem like that obnoxious salesperson when you don't know who your services are for and if your potential clients will find them valuable. It's as if you're asking a stranger if they want to buy your services. Like a person standing on the street and handing out flyers, no one wants to accept what you're offering. And that's when sell becomes a four-letter word. You are not this person!

You've probably heard that sales is about relationships. This is true. So you must begin by forming relationships with your potential clients. You do this to genuinely get to know the other person. Even when the person is your ideal client, you'll have the advantage of knowing they are right for you. However, they don't know you are right for them. Once you have established a relationship with them, you earn the right and permission to offer your services. Not before. Timing is everything. You can only know the right timing if you have the proper relationship.

The bottom line is if you think selling is bad, you need to shift your mindset. Find the place where you believe with everything in you that your ideal clients need what you have. You're providing a valuable service. Your clients are fortunate to have you working for them. If you don't believe this, why should they?

We also avoid selling, even under the right circumstances, to avoid being hurt by rejection. When we experience rejection—the no's or, even worse, the crickets—it hurts. Much like failure, rejection stings.

Also much like failure, you can't escape rejection. Both are a part of life and business. But there are some things you can do to make sure you handle rejection better. Dr. Gladys Ato, author of *The Good Goodbye*, says it's all about how you shape the rejection during your self-talk. We typically have a tendency to place blame—blaming yourself for what you could have done better or blaming the other party. It's a normal part of coping.

Dr. Ato reminds us how our minds will begin to imagine things if we don't get answers to our questions. It is extremely important to remember the big picture. It's not easy to find an opportunity for reasons not yet understood, but it's crucial.

In Dr. Ato's own experience while writing her book, missing deadlines was a form of rejection. Originally her book was scheduled to be released in January 2016. Instead it was released in October 2017, which turned out to be the perfect time. I myself couldn't agree more.

I discovered her through our mutual friend Cary Hokama. Dr. Ato appeared on Cary's podcast in August 2016. Also at just the right time. I might not have ever befriended her if the sting of rejection caused her to give up or think the right time had passed her by. You have to create the right story when you face rejection and believe it's an opportunity for you to go in another direction.

In 2016 I thought I wanted to begin speaking more often. I've enjoyed being on panels and hosting events. To me, it was the natural next step in my career. However, when conferences came up, I was never chosen to be a speaker. It felt like a crushing blow, and naturally I blamed myself for the rejection. Eventually I gave up and thought maybe speaking wasn't right for me. Now I know it wasn't for me, but for reasons I couldn't have known yet. If I had been chosen to speak at any of those events, I couldn't have traveled the world in 2017!

Sometimes we fear rejection so much that we feel rejected without reason. No one can reject you if you don't ask for what you want. If your consultation process never makes an ask to work with your potential client, it's not rejection. You simply had a nice informational chat.

Many virtual assistants have told me they don't like asking for money. That's understandable. However, you're not simply asking for money. You're not selling raffle tickets or magazine subscriptions. You are providing a service for which you should be paid. This isn't volunteer work. When you are working with your ideal clients and providing exactly what they want, they are happy to pay you.

You are the answer to someone's need. There is nothing wrong with getting paid to fill the need. You got paid as an employee for serving and meeting the needs of others. Now you are doing the same for your own clients. What pain will they thank you for taking away? So first things first, ask.

- **You should only ask your ideal clients.** If you ask 50 of the wrong potential clients, you might get one "yes." It won't feel good though. That law of averages will be very draining. It also doesn't help you. Even when you don't earn new business, you should learn something from the experience. The wrong clients won't have any useful feedback to share with you, yet it won't stop them from sharing. If you're going to get 49 "no's," you had better learn a lot of lessons! I can promise you that getting 49 rejections from the right clients is easily fixed!

- **Create a game plan for how you are going to deal with rejection.** I like to think of it as a resiliency plan. Resiliency allows people to bounce back quickly after setbacks. How do you become more resilient? Keep good company. There once was a time when rejection seemed like my shadow. I was able to keep getting out of bed and keep going—when in the back of my mind I was wondering how much more rejection I could take—by surrounding myself with women who supported me. They challenged me to keep trying and gave me tips on what I could do differently. These women shared their own stories with me. Ultimately, these women laughed and celebrated with me. I don't know where I'd be today if not for them.

- **Figure out what you have learned from the rejection.** There is always something to learn. When you learn something, rejection can be a gift. In fact, being rejected is how I created the business I have now. If not for meeting so many people who didn't need my VA services, I never would have known they needed my matchmaking services instead. These were my 49 "no's" from the right clients. Lesson learned. Problem solved!

Goal Setting

Salespeople and business owners have goals. You're both a salesperson and a business owner, so you need to have goals as well. They are *your* goals. No one else's. Don't dream of fancy cars, boats, and vacation homes if that is not your desire. Few things are worse than killing yourself to make someone else's dream your reality.

In the beginning I was told to list out my financial goals but to start with no less than six figures. We already had a problem. I'd never made six figures in my life. I was struggling to make ends meet, and I was told that six figures should be my goal? Why don't I just add a unicorn to my Christmas list too?

Goals are for *you*. You have to believe, in the midst of doubt and fear, that what you want is absolutely achievable. You have to be willing to work harder and take calculated risks because your goals are that important to you. Your actions have to be tied to a real goal not a pipe dream.

When I got honest with myself and knew exactly what I believed I was capable of, it changed the course of my business. Not only was it easier, it became *easy*. All of a sudden, I couldn't imagine not getting paid what I was worth because I wouldn't have taken any office job for less. Why in the world would I work for myself for less? Suddenly I realized I had been thinking backwards.

Goal setting can be very powerful when done right. When done wrong, it becomes demoralizing. When you set your goals, they should be very specific and they should light a fire in you. You become bound and determined to make them a reality. Not only was making six figures at the time seemingly impossible, but $100,000 represented nothing to me. Even today when I think about how much money I want to make, it's only after I know where the money will be coming from and how it will be used in both my business and my personal life.

I have no desires for cars or homes and felt such relief when I got rid of both to travel the world. Traveling the world wasn't always a dream for me. In fact, most of my life I was terrified to fly. Once I realized I was no longer afraid to fly, the first thing I did was apply for my passport. That was in May of 2015. In June 2015 my passport was delivered, and I began planning the trip of a lifetime to Nice, France, for the Monaco Grand Prix in 2016.

I was very specific as I planned it all out. I didn't simply dream of going one day. When I began planning the trip a year in advance, I wasn't even earning what I do today. However, I knew I was going to make it work somehow, and I did. Nothing was charged to debt, and the trip was paid for before I left. I had even calculated my spending money.

When you're taking the right steps toward your goals, you'll open yourself up to more than you ever thought. My first international trip turned out not to be to Nice in May 2016. Instead it happened five months earlier in December 2015 when I spent New Year's Eve in London. I even got to fly first class! When my goal became to take my first international trip, international travel also became a gift.

Only two international trips in and that was it—my goals changed again. I didn't want to travel internationally once or possibly twice a year. I wanted to travel constantly. I wanted to make it my next goal more than anything. Eventually I discovered We Roam, an organization that coordinates trips around the world for people like me—remote workers who love to travel. After only three months of making this my new goal, I became a part of We Roam's first group to travel the world for a year while working. The tour was 12 countries in 12 months, and I managed to sneak in a few extra for a total of 16 countries in a single year! That's the power of goal setting. And this all happened while I experienced another record year in business.

Your goals shouldn't be like mine unless they already are. When I first started, all I wanted was to be at home when my daughter needed me. It was fantastic. I was able to be with my family in all situations. That was my dream, and I made it come true. After becoming an empty nester, my goals changed. And my goals have continued to change. The point is you cannot want someone else's dream for yourself.

Think about your goals. Write down at least three—one immediate, one short-term, and one long-term. Next write a dollar amount by each one. How much money will it take to accomplish each goal? Don't guess; be very specific. If your dream is buying a new car, research it and figure out exactly what it will cost, even including insurance. If your dream is to send your children to a private school or to pay their college tuition, determine what that tuition is, calculate book fees and other miscellaneous costs, uniforms, and even transportation costs. After you have done this work, then you can begin to believe in the prices you'll charge for your services.

Negotiations

One of the most common suggestions to help with every aspect of your business is to survey your clients and customers. Easier said than done. Companies spend millions trying to get their hands on surveys and data and then sift through it properly. You probably don't have an email list yet to survey. So how can you survey the exact people you need to? Through negotiations.

You've priced your services, you're making sales, and then there are negotiating opportunities. I actually really like negotiating. I don't change my prices. However, based on what my clients have tried to negotiate, I learned that they needed more options. Negotiating with them on services and pricing allowed me to create tiered options. It's another instance when your ideal clients will tell you everything you need to know.

There are several rules to successful negotiations. First, always look for the win-win situation. If you're trying to come out on top, that's not negotiating. That's competing. Few people are more competitive than I. However, if you're winning in business, you have to ask yourself who is losing. My clients aren't losers. I don't compete with them. Negotiate with your clients so you both can be winners.

Negotiations are another crucial way to learn more about your ideal client—what they want, what they will pay for, and how you can better position yourself to meet their needs. Through consultation discussions, you'll know what your clients want and need. Don't assume they are negotiating your price. This is a common mistake. Also, don't assume the client will know how to begin negotiations. You may have to begin the process.

Let's say your potential client really wants to work with you, and you really want to work with them. Your calendar isn't full of clients yet, so you can be flexible. After the consultation, your potential client tells you he or she doesn't have the money to pay for your services or can't afford you. These are cues to continue the conversation.

If they don't have the money, it means their business isn't off the ground yet. Or they could be waiting on a few contracts to come in. Don't assume. Ask which it is. Then suggest a date and a time to follow up in the future, hopefully at a time when they will have more cash flow.

If they can't afford you, ask what they were expecting to pay. If it's not even in the ballpark, ask if they would pay more if they could afford it. You need to be a bit bold because you'll never have the opportunity to ask such important questions to a more perfect audience.

It's rare you'll get an actual figure of what the client was expecting to pay. At this point, you probably haven't created your tiered services, which is completely normal. It's only after you go through many consultations and negotiations that you know what sells and what doesn't. However, *any* information a potential client gives you can be used to your advantage.

I have three tiered options for matchmaking. The two lower packages only solidify my top tier package. In the end, what the client said they wanted, they actually didn't. They just didn't know it until I laid it out and told them how much work they'd be doing.

When you negotiate down, you can only lower your price if you lower your services. In some instances, this will be exactly what your client is looking for. In other cases, once the client knows what they won't be getting, they'll opt to figure out how to afford you. **Never lower your price and keep the services the same.** You'll dig yourself a hole you can't get out of, also known as a grave.

There is always the chance the client is misunderstanding their needs and what you provide. During the negotiation process, make sure the client speaks more than you do. Keep track of what they're saying. Repeat back what you heard and weave your services into the conversation appropriately. One use of a word or different verbiage on your part could lead them down the wrong path. Using the client's own verbiage is the quickest way to get them on your side. The negotiation process will also help you refine how you speak with your ideal clients.

How do you know if you have negotiated successfully? Ask yourself how your client wins and how you win. If you can't answer in a positive way for both of you, keep at it until you can.

Trust me, you will come across people who think they are going to pay you $7 an hour for all of your top-notch services. End that conversation immediately. Don't entertain those types of conversations. It seems harsh, but you need to show value in every way possible. Continuing a conversation with someone who wants to pay you less than minimum wage shows you don't value yourself. Remember, you don't need the world to hire you; you only need a few clients. Throw that fish back.

Contracts

VAs use contracts to protect ourselves and our clients. But avoid using extremely negative verbiage. Think of your contract as a prenuptial agreement. You're both excited to begin working together. You've got all the warm and fuzzy feelings. Now you're sending documents that outline what's yours and what's theirs—all the breakup terms. Be mindful of what is standard contract verbiage and what is too much. You don't want to scare the client and put them in a frame of mind that things *will* go wrong before they've even started working with you. If you feel that extra need to protect yourself, you probably shouldn't begin working with this client.

Your contract should be a formality. It shouldn't be the first place where your clients find out what you'll do for them, what you won't do for them, when and how they can reach you, your time-off policy, and how you get paid. Those conversations should take place when you and the client agree to work together. Your contract is simply a recap of what you've already spoken about together.

You can find many free contracts online through a variety of websites. However, I suggest connecting with your local chamber of commerce or city/state small business associations. They can serve as great resources to any new VA.

Three Ways to Gain Confidence as a Virtual Assistant

Being a business owner is a lot like dating. I like to use dating as a metaphor because it's all about attracting and building relationships with the right people and getting rid of the duds. Whether or not you're in the dating phase of life, it's something we all can relate to. And we've all seen someone go about it the wrong way. Here are three ways to improve your confidence level as a new VA:

- **Believe in what you're selling**. When you're dating, through your actions you try to show the other person what a great catch you are. If you spend the entire date talking about all of your flaws or worse, you share what others thought your flaws were, the person probably isn't going to ask you out again. The same is true in business. If you start out by saying you haven't been doing this for very long, you *hope* things work out, you share your *bad* client stories, and you tell me you aren't very busy, I'm not likely to call again either. People want to date and do business with people who are in demand. Period.

- **Believe in your value.** If someone takes you to McDonald's for a date, how much do you think they value you? If you agree to eat there, how much do you value yourself? No one is going to treat you better than you treat yourself. The same is true with your clients. Some clients will try to pay you pennies for your work. Run as fast as you can from them! You don't want them or their friends. Don't engage in a conversation or even try to explain why you charge more. Build your confidence by remembering this client wants to date you at McDonald's. It helps put things in perspective. Not everyone can afford your services, and that is fine. You're still valuable. The goal is to find the clients who can afford you and to provide so much value that they'll continue working with you in the future!

- **Believe in your most attractive quality.** The Law of Attraction is real. We attract people who are like us. If you keep attracting the wrong client, think about the signals you are sending out. If they don't want to pay your fees, are you somehow implying your services are cheap? Does your website or social media profiles scream "bargain basement?" Are you trying to attract filet mignon at Burger King? If your clients are too demanding and crossing boundaries, have you positioned yourself to be their partner in business or do you portray yourself as a secretary from *Mad Men*? Your ideal client is drawn to you because you get them. Attract them by speaking their language in a way that only you can.

"Dating" potential clients can be rough in the beginning. And yes, you might have to go through some bad dates and bad clients. But your ideal one is out there!

Is Your Business Worth Your Time?

Starting a business doesn't have to be hard. It doesn't *have* to be, but it can often feel that way. Running a business requires you to do things you don't want to do. Wearing multiple hats is a necessity that will challenge you in the most unexpected of ways. However, the most common challenge new virtual assistants experience is getting clients, otherwise referred to as sales.

It can be daunting to do the thing you absolutely despise the most—sales—when you need it the most to pay the bills and enjoy the freedom you dream of. The most common remedy VAs have to this problem is to get a part-time job. I understand the need to pay bills and take care of your family. But there is a flaw in this plan.

The flaw is your mental attitude. You see, you have just decided another person's company is more important than your own. So much so that you are willing to devote to someone else the precious time you could be spending on phone calls, email messages, and networking with potential clients. Yes, you'll get a paycheck, but you won't create a business.

Getting clients is your number one priority when you first begin as a virtual assistant. Nothing is more important because clients keep you in business. Using the excuse that you're not good at sales won't cut it. When VAs tell me they're struggling, one of the things I ask them is how much of their day is spent making calls, emails, and connections. Most often it is less than an hour a day. I'm sure it seems much longer because it is something they don't enjoy doing, but if this is your business, shouldn't it be worth your time?

Wishing, hoping, and praying are great ways to raise your spirits. But that's not a strategic plan to grow your business. What if your potential client was using this same method to pay you? It would be unacceptable. Recently I read Chris Spurvey's book *It's Time to Sell*, and it was a game changer. Not only is it a great book to help you sell your VA services, but I encourage you to take advantage of Chris's knowledge. He has sold more than $300 million in consulting services, and he can help you make a strategic plan for free if you visit his website, www.chrisspurvey.com.

The time is now. Give your business your best. Give your business your time. Do the hard work now, and one day it won't seem so hard.

Summary

- Now you know how and why to price your services. You cannot sell services without knowing what you charge and what your value is. Pricing is not a competition. You have the ability to stay nimble. In the same manner that you can change your services, you also can change your prices.

- You've learned the importance of having the right mindset to sell yourself. Get comfortable selling because it's not a bad word. Don't shy away from it because when you do, it shows a lack of confidence. When you believe in what you're offering, you'll know you're doing your ideal clients a favor.

- You know the best way to collect payment, negotiate, and create a contract in order to create a win-win situation for you and your clients. Remember, you're not in business to be the only winner because this means your client would have to be the loser. You know that offering more services in the beginning confuses your ideal client.

Now that we've laid the foundation and you're ready to take on clients, in the next chapter we are going to cover how to master the consultation.

CHAPTER 4

Step 4: Mastering the Consultation

I decided to make this a chapter all its own to highlight the importance of mastering the consultation. You've done all the work to get to this point and yet here is where I see the hard work of so many being lost. Few things set the expectations and tone of a working relationship like the consultation process. At the end of the consultation, the potential client should view you as an expert in your field.

First let's discuss the difference between a sales call and a consultation. A sales call is all about the product or service you're selling. The customer already knows what it is and possibly how much it costs. Your job on a sales call is to collect payment. You might ask or answer a few questions to close the deal, but the potential customer is controlling the conversation. That is a sales call. To close deals over the phone, you need to have a lot of sales calls. I'm not a fan of sales calls. If you list your prices on your website, you'll have more sales calls than consultations.

A consultation is something entirely different. Now I've had people call these "discovery calls," "get to know you conversations," and just about everything in between. I choose to call mine "consultations" because the term is universally understood.

Just remember that you control your consultations. Steer the conversations in the way they should go. This is how you help the client. A consultation, whether or not the person hires you, should be enlightening. Your job is to share information, valuable information the client does not have yet.

Start at the beginning—it's simple but important. Ask the person how he or she found you. Ask what he or she knows about you and your services. The potential client should know some basic information before you start. Also be sure that the process is clear. Your potential client should understand what will happen during the consultation and after so you aren't wasting anyone's time.

In your complimentary workbook, you'll find a copy of the exact consultation form I use. The key is to think of yourself as a therapist. Ask a question and then shut your mouth. Don't offer your help and don't try to finish the other person's sentence. And avoid reframing the question. You need to give the person time to think. Some answers will fly off their tongues while others stump them.

One thing you'll notice on my consultation form is that some of the questions are vague. That's on purpose. When I ask a client how they measure success and they start with the VA, I know they are more worried about the VA's work than their own. If they begin with themselves, I know they are already in a better frame of mind to start working with a VA. If they ask me to whom I'm referring them, I'll let them answer for either or both. This lets me know they don't appreciate vagueness. They want both parties to be successful, and they know the measurements are not the same. All of this is extremely valuable information.

The timing of the consultation is also the same as a therapist session, about 45 minutes. Are some consultations shorter? Of course. However, I don't want to rush the person or not be able to give my full attention to them because I'm worried about running into my next meeting time. The consultation is not about you. It's about the potential client.

When the consultation is over, I invite the potential client to share anything I've missed. Sometimes they will add to or refine a previous response. Sometimes they will be ready to end the consultation. The point is, you must let the client say everything they need to before it's your turn to talk.

Based on the responses you receive, make your recommendation to the potential client. Include details about the work you will complete, deadlines, and what the client can expect from working with you. Explain what the process will look like and how long it will take to complete. Use the client's words back to them. Remember, this isn't about you. When you repeat the client's words, you let him or her know you have truly heard them, speak their language, and haven't changed the meaning of what they said.

Ask the client how he or she would like to begin your working relationship. Gather as much information as you can at the consultation so you have everything you need to successfully start when the client is ready.

Finally, state your fee. Then go silent and let the potential client respond. Do not speak first! Especially, in the beginning because you'll be tempted to discount your own prices.

If a client wants to work with you, follow these next steps:

- Before you end the consultation, collect the information you need or set an appointment for when it can be collected. Yes, this is before you receive any payment. You don't have to start working yet, but you need to have something to work with.

- Let the client know how you'll be working together—working hours, communication standards, upcoming holidays or time off, and how you collect payment. Of course, this information also will be in your contract, but there shouldn't be any surprises for your client. It's better to speak about the contract now than exchange emails back and forth later.

- Email the contract within 24 hours of your consultation. It's even better if you can send it by the end of the same day. No matter how many services you offer, you should have a standard contract or template ready to go at all times.

- Invoicing should be done at the same time you send the contract. Many software platforms allow you to do this seamlessly.

- Make sure the client knows the work begins when you receive the payment.

- Before you end the consultation, set an appointment for your first check-in (within one week of your beginning the work). You will need to confirm that you're doing what the client expects from you.

What if the client is unsure? That's fair. You don't hire everyone immediately.

- Make a follow-up appointment before you end the consultation. At the very least, ask permission to reach out to him or her on a specific day. Remember, these are busy people who feel like they don't have enough time now. How much time will they have later to talk to you again?

- Send a follow-up email by the end of the day, recapping what you spoke about during your consultation—the services that will best fit their needs, how you can be reached, and your fees.

- Provide a bonus, something that would be valuable to the potential client. It could be a graphic, your favorite eBook on something you discussed during the consultation, or some tips for success in their industry. Give something of value. No email signup required!

What if the client wants referrals?

- Send them! Don't be the person who feels like they don't have to send referrals to potential clients. If you're taking on new clients, you can afford the courtesy of providing references.

- What if you don't have any? Use references from previous employers or from volunteer work.

- If you don't have either of those, offer to do some kind of test for the potential client—a short-term project to determine if you both would be a good fit for working together. Be honest and transparent. That is the character all potential clients are looking for.

Journaling

I'm a huge fan of journaling. It's a part of my daily life and my business life. As you start out on this journey of building your VA business, I highly recommend journaling. Document and compare every consultation you have to look for similarities and differences. Who are your potential clients, and who are your paid clients? What differentiates them? Find every difference and every similarity you can. Look beyond the work and the field. You'll find it to be eye-opening.

My matchmaking clients and my private clients are total opposites. I didn't realize this until I started looking through the documentation of my consultation appointments. It was painfully obvious. You will only find what you look for, so make a point to look for similarities and differences.

On the same note, you should journal to look for wins. You would think wins would be easy to spot, but you'd be wrong! One year as I reviewing what I journaled during the previous year, I couldn't recognize my own thinking. I wrote about something that upset me, but now I couldn't relate to that emotion anymore. The new me no longer got upset by such things. The win was growing my business mindset.

In another entry, I wrote how excited I was to get a new contract, a contract I wouldn't walk across the street for now. In fact, as I was reading this old entry, I had recently signed another contract with the same company for literally thousands of dollars more. This time I wasn't excited. I simply was happy to have kept the client through raising my prices, but the excitement was gone. What a horrible mistake that was. Not only did I almost miss the win, I almost took it for granted!

You need to celebrate your wins. Every win. Every win won't be monumental, but you do have to recognize them. As a business owner, you will have days where you feel defeated, exhausted, or just plain tired. Going days, weeks, and months without recognizing your wins will cause burnout.

Another benefit to journaling is that things are not always as bad as they seem if you get them down on paper. If you play scenarios over and over in your mind, things can always seem to get worse. Journaling is therapeutic.

You don't have to journal a lot. Start off with a one-line-a-day journal. Anyone can write one good thing a day! You may find your one thing is being able to make it to your child's event, being able to take care of a loved one, joining a class that takes place in the middle of the day. A win is a win. Write it down and celebrate it.

Summary

- Now you are prepared to master your own consultation. Use the form I shared in your workbook to create a consultation that is specific to your ideal clients. Remember, you set the tone and expectations for the working relationship during the consultation.

- You've learned the importance of journaling to look for patterns and to celebrate your wins. We find what we look for, and sometimes we can miss or forget what is right in front of us. Use a journal as a positive tool to grow your business mindset.

Now you're ready to begin networking and targeting your ideal client. Networking and searching out clients before you laid the foundation and know how to conduct a consultation is like buying a car and then learning how to drive. I love to network, so I am especially excited about the next chapter!

CHAPTER 5

Step 5: Networking and Targeting Your Ideal Client

I have yet to meet a VA who didn't gain his or her first client from their existing circle of associates. However, that is only the beginning. Networking will lead you to multiple clients and a steady stream of referrals, helping you stay relevant and become better known. There are other perks to networking, such as being asked to join boards, giving back to your community in ways you didn't know you could, collaborating with peers in your field, and so on. Networking changed my life and opened doors that made an entirely new life possible.

The key to networking is having a plan. If there's one thing I know about admins it's that we like to have plans!

Most people will tell you to get out of your comfort zone—step out and everything will be fine. I disagree. In the beginning of starting your business, it's important to have a safe space where you feel comfortable taking calculated risks.

Networking is a calculated risk because the groups you join should require a fee. When you join a free group, there is less of a vested interest among its members. Since many of your clients pay for services and resources related to running their businesses, you should do the same. It will remind you that the group is an investment and should be treated as such. When you spend money on networking, you'll be more selective about the groups you join as well. You want to be selective and think not only of your ideal client but the impact that group can have on you and your business.

Networking, like building client relationships, is about the long game. To start, you should join three carefully selected groups. I was fortunate to be able to network in person when I first started my VA business. I attended every networking event people invited me to. When someone suggested I might find clients at XYZ event, I agreed, even when they didn't know who my ideal client was. Huge mistake!

I only had myself to blame. When I first started, I didn't know who my ideal client was, and I found myself running around like a chicken with its head cut off. I was spending tons of time, energy, resources, and money networking with all the wrong people, in all the wrong places. To say I was drained would be an understatement.

It didn't click until I went to an event and someone told me I was in the wrong place. As I sat in my car and cried, I processed every feeling I had. Frustration, anger, embarrassment, humiliation, disappointment, and fear. Then I asked myself how the man behind the table knew I wasn't at the right event. He knew I didn't belong there because the event was full of his ideal clients, and he immediately recognized I wasn't one of them.

What he said hurt my feelings, but if I could go back and thank him, I would. Sitting there in my car, crying and feeling like a failure, I vowed this would never happen again. Never again would I attend an event based on another person's suggestion. Never again would I go where my ideal clients were not. If I went to an event and it wasn't the right fit, fine. But I was going to do my homework first.

Always remember to go where your clients are. It's very frustrating to network with people who aren't a good fit for you. It's not fun for them either. You should be asking yourself if your ideal client is in this group. If so, is there more than one of them there?

With networking, you have to give it time. I know people who will not purposely work with someone who comes to an event only once or twice.

They want to do business with people who are regulars and who want to build relationships. Some want to refer someone to you, but they won't because they're not sure if they'll ever see you again and they wonder if you'll still be in business a few months from now. My rule of thumb is to join a carefully selected group where I think my ideal clients are, then dedicate a solid year to it.

I originally joined the National Association of Women Business Owners (NAWBO) because it seemed like a safe place to learn about business. A place where I could be free to be vulnerable with other women, ask the "embarrassing" questions. A space where women were committed to helping one another. Almost a year after I joined, I signed my first contract as a direct result of the group. The contract was for more than 2,000 percent of my annual fee and the largest contract I had signed up to that time. The woman who recommended me for this contract did so because she knew she could count on me. I was a regular, reliable, and dependable member of the group.

I highly encourage you to choose in-person groups for your first three networking groups. We'll talk about online groups later, but I believe there is no substitute for being in the same room as other people. Also, most business people believe they can judge a person's character and knowledge within the first few minutes of meeting you. This process takes much longer online.

I'll share a secret with you. The number of VAs who network in person is very small. Frequently I'm the only VA in the groups where I'm a member. Who do you think gets every referral when someone needs a virtual assistant?

Each of your first three networking groups should have a distinct purpose. You must know your expectations for each group. Then determine if you have the time to commit to the group. No group, no matter how fantastic, will allow you to reap benefits unless you commit to putting forth an effort to create relationships. As you choose your three networking groups, consider one of these purposes for each group:

Group 1: Support

The very first group I joined was NAWBO. I knew how to be an assistant; what I didn't know was how to run a business. And that's where NAWBO came in.

Joining NAWBO was easily one of the best business decisions I ever made. Without the support of other women in business, in a safe space, learning best practices, I would not be in business today. NAWBO not only provided resources to me, but it also gave me a group of accountability partners, women to lift me up when I was down and provide actionable advice and—my favorite part—help me celebrate my wins!

Did I get clients and referrals out of the group? Yes. However, that was secondary to me. Networking within NAWBO was highly profitable. Whenever you network the right way, you should reap benefits. If I used this group mainly for sales, I might have gotten frustrated and might have left before getting that big contract.

Group 2: Clients

Where can you find your clients? That's where you need to be. Choose a networking group where you can find potential clients. And consider your client's schedule. If your potential clients are moms, they are most likely going to meet in the morning or over lunch hours. For them, late afternoons and evenings are spent picking up kids, attending practices, preparing dinner, and spending time with family. When you investigate a networking group, be sure its goals and events cater to your ideal client and his or her schedule.

Think about the options the group offers for meeting other members. Luncheons are nice, but that can mean quick networking sessions at the beginning and sitting around during the meal. Then people are running out the door to head to their next meeting. Happy hours can be fun, but again, make sure this suits your ideal client's schedule.

My favorite groups are those with roundtable events and open discussion forums. You not only learn from and hear the frustrations of your ideal clients, you also get to hear their language, what's important to them in doing business, and how they want to make a difference. Listening is key.

Another component is sharing. You might find it difficult to share at first but be patient. Inevitably someone is going to bring up a topic that is your area of expertise. This is your chance to speak with authority and provide value. This is how you get people to know, like, and trust you. You also create curiosity, which is how you open up the lines of communication and make connections.

Group 3: Community

A community group could be your local government, a charitable organization, or even a sports group. In a community group, you are connecting with other people who share your same goals or passions. Being a part of a community group is important because as you start your business, you tend to focus inwardly. It's natural to forget what really matters in the grand scheme of things when you spend your time building a business. So you use a community group to help you put things in perspective. You'll find yourself refreshed and renewed with a positive outlook on life after attending these group events.

I've been pleasantly surprised at the caliber of people I've meet in my community groups, people I had no chance of meeting otherwise. Organizing an event, hosting a fundraiser, and working at the snack bar together were like mini-business courses. And other members of my community groups were very intrigued by what I was doing, causing them to be more than willing to tell others about me and my business.

Networking is all about stretching yourself to make new friends. By joining three specific groups, you've taken a lot of the guesswork out of networking because you know what to expect from each group. Still, it can be a little intimidating. Change your mindset and the process will become much easier. Make it your goal to meet two interesting people who are creating a new course. Or someone who just hired another team member. Think about what your ideal client might be sharing. When your goal is to meet interesting people, it makes it much easier to have a conversation.

One of my girlfriends works in sales. When she attends networking events, she always has a specific goal in mind. It's never to make a sale. She knows it's not going to happen right now at this event. Making the sale is for when she is sitting in their office several months down the road. Right now, she is looking to meet someone very specific. She looks at her goals and decides where she's going to focus her attention during that networking event. By the time she finishes a glass of wine while networking, she knows that she needs to make at least two solid connections with people she can follow up with. She cannot enjoy another glass of wine or go home until she meets her goal.

This might not be the best strategy when you first begin your business, but the point is you need to have a strategy. If you don't plan to meet and connect with anyone, you won't. Plain and simple. Much like creating your ideal client, when you have it in your head who you're going to meet, the person appears in front of you.

Yes, You Need to Have an Elevator Pitch

I'm sure you've heard the term "elevator pitch." It means being able to summarize you and your business in just a few seconds. Having an elevator pitch isn't just for entrepreneurs who are raising seed money or making an important presentation. Thanks to these entrepreneurs, we now know the clarity an elevator pitch can bring to your business.

What if you're not asking for anything? What if the person you're speaking to isn't even a potential client? Do you really need to have an elevator pitch? Yes! As a virtual assistant, your elevator pitch isn't only for the client you're speaking with. It's also so people can refer you to others with complete confidence. Not only are they referring people to you, with the right pitch they are referring your *ideal clients* to you.

You may have the opportunity to explain your business to someone in person. However, if you have to explain it, how can someone else quickly refer you? They won't. Chances are they won't even remember you and your business because it's too much information to take in. Remember, at networking events the goal is to meet your ideal client. You only have a few moments to share information. Your elevator pitch will help you do this the right way.

I've heard a lot of virtual assistants explain what they do instead of mentioning their client. The key is to combine both the ideal client or industry with your specific skills sets and unique values. Otherwise even if you stand out, the client is still unsure if they are right for you. Your elevator pitch should include your potential clients' problems and how you can solve those problems with your services. When you describe your clients in this way, they will recognize you are the right choice for them.

Those who don't truly understand the pitch process have ruined it for all of us. It seems like everyone is pitching you something every time you turn the corner. In most cases, it's awful. The ones I despise the most are those who inflate their pitches. You know the ones. *I work with exceptional world class leaders who are ready to take their businesses to the next level. Or I work with multipotentialites who are in the top of their field and are ready to break through their ceiling to discover their true potential.* They kind of make me want to put my finger down my throat.

Your elevator pitch isn't just for your client. It's for everyone you come into contact with while networking. It should be so simple that it can be repeated easily. You want the person you are speaking with to understand your business and then repeat what they hear to others. You never know when the person you're speaking with will meet your ideal client. You want that person to immediately realize, *you could really benefit from this VA's services.* If you can master your elevator pitch, you will create referrals.

Your elevator pitch paints a picture of you and your business, just like your client avatar and your niche create an image for yourself. You're not eliminating potential clients; you're narrowing in on your ideal client. Oh, how I struggled my way through this one! Being simple and concise is an art. If you struggle in this area, as I did, sharing your elevator pitch as much as possible will give you the critical feedback you need.

Have you ever heard a bad elevator pitch? What was bad about it? If someone has a bad reaction to your elevator pitch, find out why. Ask the person what they think it is you do and who they believe your client is. Some people will offer this up to you without asking. It's how I became a "matchmaker."

At first I referred to myself as a "staffer." Part of my pitch was that I find the right virtual assistant. However, those I networked with casually said, "Oh, so you're like a matchmaker." When you hear something often, take notice. I decided I could either embrace this idea or change my focus. Matchmaking was the perfect word picture to describe what I do.

Here are some examples of clear and concise elevator pitches. They let potential clients know exactly what you do and to whom you provide the service. Don't be scared to be very specific! That is the goal of a good elevator pitch.

I am a lead page expert for coaches who want to have a higher conversion rate on their lead magnets.

I create online courses for professionals who can no longer take on one-on-one clients.

I manage product launches for online entrepreneurs who are looking to grow their audiences.

I'm an executive virtual assistant for busy professionals who can no longer manage to get everything done.

Your clients can identify with these statements very easily. After hearing your elevator pitch, your potential client should know they are your ideal client. Your words say exactly what they want to hear.

If you try to create an elevator pitch that speaks to everyone, it will never attract *the one*. That's because your pitch is too generic. It doesn't matter if you do more than just the one task you mention in your pitch. You don't have to describe all of your services. Those things will be implied.

You will have far better results when you are concise. Take a look at almost any VA's website. They all say pretty much the same thing—*I will save you time and money. I don't have overhead expenses. I can work from anywhere.* I know. I was a huge offender. But none of these pitches speaks specifically to any one client.

Create your elevator pitch then start using it with your networking groups. This will help you get over any fears and prepare you for the day you pitch to large companies. Remember, the longer you hold on to something without trying it, the more frightening it becomes.

Find a Networking Partner

Some of my NAWBO sisters and I have fun networking together. For one, it's comforting to see a familiar face in the room when you're nervous. Second, it's a great way to make introductions.

Inevitably, through networking you will meet someone who is not a good fit for your business but is perfect for one of your partners. That's when it's so important to have a networking partner—you can talk up your partner to someone who needs his or her services, and they can return the favor for you.

Your networking partner also can serve as an accountability partner. You can't be a wallflower when you're being watched at a networking event. You can't duck out early, and you can't merely float around the room. You have to become part of the conversation. When you have someone in the room you're accountable to, you'll be more diligent about accomplishing this goal.

Networking In Person

You can't keep in touch without business cards. Don't assume you don't need them because you're virtual. Everyone needs business cards. Consider yourself unprepared if you don't have this crucial business tool. Having a digital business card is another best practice. Put your information in your own contact list. Then when you meet someone and they want to immediately connect with you, send them a contact share. You'll also be able to fit much more on a digital business card than on a printed one.

Don't make it your goal to collect business cards at networking events. In fact, I try to accept cards only from people I want to form relationships with, and I never offer my card to a random person. Each card you collect requires a follow-up. Having to follow up with 20 random people is exhausting.

You should follow up with your networking contacts within 24 hours of meeting them. And your follow-up should be personal. Include where and when you met. Just because you're following up within 24 hours doesn't mean your contact will read your message before attending another event. Remind them who you are. Let them know why you might want to keep in touch and include something of value to them. Here's an example of a successful follow-up email. Don't forget to think about the subject line!

Subject line: Thanks for introducing me to Jane Smith

Body: Joe, it was a pleasure meeting you yesterday at my first XYZ event. I appreciate your taking the time to introduce me to Jane, who is an ideal client for me. We have a meeting scheduled for next week already! Please let me know how I can be of assistance to you in the future.

BTW—You mentioned that you are going to hire an in-person assistant to replace your longtime assistant who is retiring. I'm happy to post the position on my admin forums to increase your talent pool with experienced executive assistants.

Have a great weekend, and I look forward to seeing you at the next XYZ event.

You easily can tailor this message any number of ways. Keep in mind these key ingredients:

- Keep it brief.

- Don't send anything they didn't ask for.

- Don't send anything that isn't valuable to them.

- Create a specific subject line.

- Remind them how you met.

- Remind them of you and who your ideal client is.

- Offer assistance in the future or now, depending on what is appropriate.

These are examples of in-person networking, something I do a good bit of in the United States. There are also plenty of ways to network online.

Networking Online

First and foremost, if you're not hanging out where your clients are online, you're losing money. Your online presence is a must so you can learn how others perceive you online.

There are many different online platforms where you can seek out potential clients. Make sure you are where they are. LinkedIn is my favorite platform, and my clients like it too. What is your title in your online profiles? How will you be found online? What will people see when they find you?

Again, don't confuse your potential client. If they are looking for a VA, are you the one they're looking for? Does your profile headline include "virtual assistant," "consultant," or "business manager?" What do these titles do? How do they benefit your client? If you truly do all of those things, can they be combined and simplified?

What you call yourself is important. I don't work with freelancers, consultants, online business managers, or the like. I work with assistants, and there is a difference.

Consultants don't do the work. They only tell you what work needs to be done. Consultants are known leaders in their fields. People actually pay for their thoughts. Are you a known leader? Is anyone paying you for your thoughts? This usually comes later in your career, not at the beginning.

Freelancers are not the same as VAs. They often can be in-person contractors. Freelancers attend meetings, make in-person pitches, or may take on only one client at a time.

Online business managers are questionable. Middle management? Who needs it? If you're going to be using that title, you need to think about how your ideal client views the term "manager."

Does your online presence, including your title, confuse your client? Be honest. If you don't have any clients, the answer is yes.

After you create your online title, think about your online photo. This isn't about judging a book by its cover. This is making a first impression. If you were meeting a potential client for the first time, is your online profile photo a good representation of the person you want them to meet? Are you smiling? Is the photo of good quality? Is it more appropriate for an online dating site? Is it animated? Is it even you? Did you post a group photo? All of these things contribute to a potential client's first impression of you and your business.

You'll have to address these questions depending on who your client is. I have been told that my online photo is no good because I am not wearing a suit, nor am I standing in a corporate setting. Instead I am wearing casual clothes outdoors. Perfect! My clients don't tend to be corporate. In fact, they have left the corporate life. In their online photos, my clients often are outdoors, and no one is wearing a suit. Most smile, some don't. I smile because if I don't I have resting bitch face. (Look it up. It's a real thing.) Your online profile photo says a lot about you.

When online networking is done effectively, you can form true and lasting relationships. When I tell people that I have never met some of my closest friends and peers, they are surprised. I'm never sure why. It comes along with what I do. If I didn't believe you can have a good working relationship or friendship online, I wouldn't be a fan of virtual assisting. It's not the time you spend together, it's the time you listen and share together. When someone understands you, you feel like you have a relationship with them.

Networking in Online Groups

Spam is one of the most common online pet peeves for many people. People and companies trying to sell you stuff you don't need. So how do you find out what people do need without spamming them? Join the groups they belong to.

Groups, on all online platforms, are a great way to be involved, answer questions, and add value to your potential clients' businesses. Instead of wondering what your clients are thinking, you'll know for certain because they're posting questions directly related to the challenges they're facing in their businesses. What better way to help them than by providing helpful tips and answers to their questions? This is how you become known, liked, and trusted.

Online groups are also a great investment in your own business. The best groups are where you are learning as well as sharing your own knowledge. So I'm not concerned if I don't get a client out of taking an online class or joining a group. The price of admission is worth it.

How do you choose your online networking groups? First, ask yourself if you have a genuine interest in this group. If not, don't join. You must be vested financially and emotionally. This is how you give and get within the group.

Not all groups will be the right fit. That's okay. You have to try. As they say, your decision should either be a "hell yes" or a "hell no." It still doesn't guarantee success, but you'll be at peace with your decision.

I did have an online fail with a networking group. I joined a well-known author's group. As in, *New York Times* bestseller and international coach and speaker. She's got quite the following. I thought her course might be good for me to take. The investment was manageable—one client would pay for it. Plus, I was ready to be coached by her. This was a win-win situation.

Well, I never got any clients from the group. And while the group is still active, I don't participate. It proved to be the wrong fit for me. Did I learn some valuable coaching lessons? Sure. Did I make some friends? Sure. Would I do it again? Hell no! The important part is that I learned from the class and why it didn't work. Sometimes when things don't work out, it solidifies for you what is your best game plan. That's exactly what it did for me.

How could I have known from the beginning how this would be the wrong fit. Research! I researched this author, but I didn't dive deep into her following and her ultimate message. If I would have done this first, I would have found out that I don't have a connection with this author's following, and I don't believe in what she is selling. She has some great thoughts and suggestions. However, I don't believe in her enough to refer her to others. These are all signs it's a "hell no!"

Online groups aren't just about getting clients. You can't do this business thing on your own. You're going to need a strong network. Join both executive assistant and virtual assistant online groups. Some of my favorites are The Bootstrap VA Facebook group, the OrgOrg Google Group, and OfficeNinjas newsletter and in-person events.

Networking amongst your peers is a powerful tool. I've learned so much, stayed on top of my game, educated myself, and even got a few clients out of it. The power of networking in the right place not only brings you clients but also helps you refer colleagues, get the services you need, support the members in your group, and form real friendships—both online and in person.

Referrals

Don't be afraid to ask other business owners for referrals. Whenever you request a referral, you've got a 50/50 chance of a yes. But be specific in your ask, whether it's in person or by email. Remind the person how you met and briefly explain your ideal client and your services. Then ask if he or she knows anyone who needs your services. If so, can he or she connect you with that person? Remember, your referrer's name is on the line. Be prepared to share letters of recommendation or testimonies from other clients. (You can even use letters of recommendation from previous employers.) When all is said and done, don't forget to thank your referrer for his or her time and ask if there is any way you can be of assistance to them.

When you receive a referral, your first response should be to request a phone call or an in-person meeting to discuss very specifically the business matter the potential client is looking for you to meet. An email to any potential client should never simply be a link to your website. Everything should be laid out in concise detail. Address the problem they have to solve, how you can solve it, and then request a follow-up consultation to discuss the details of a potential working relationship.

Getting referrals is great. Giving referrals is even better. It's another great way to form relationships. When referring to other VAs, ask them who their ideal client is and if they are taking on new clients. Let them know who you have in mind to refer to them, make sure it's a good fit, and then ask how best to make the introduction. In turn, they'll do the same for you.

If you notice that you refer several people to one particular person or company and in turn receive a lot of referrals from the same person or company, it's time to consider a partnership. This could be in the form of an affiliate, referral perks, or having your name listed on their website as a preferred partner. Whatever the case might be, look for a way to form a partnership that adds value to both parties.

This also can be done with other VAs. Sadly, I don't see this happening often. Instead of sharing clients, another VA is brought in as a subcontractor. I don't recommend subcontracting because you don't get to choose your ideal client. You are at the mercy of being handed clients with whom you might not want to work. Contact with the client could be difficult, and there may be barriers created by the VA you are working for. Also, you lose the ability to make decisions you know are right. Your company name isn't on the contract and that is the person who gets to have the final say. Ultimately, you are leaving one 9 to 5 for another.

Another reason to avoid subcontracting is because you most likely will make less money for your work than you deserve. Think about it—the person who is subcontracting you is in the business of making money and will lower your rate to the least amount they are willing to pay. They are gathering the clients and maintaining those relationships. However, your work is the same. Are you willing to forfeit some of your income just to have steady work?

Instead of sub-contracting, think of ways your work can complement other VAs' work. There are certain virtual assistants who would be a natural fit to refer to one another. If you are an executive VA for a business coach, partner with a graphic design VA when your business coach needs a new logo or other graphics. In return, it's likely the graphic design VA can refer you to one of his or her own clients who needs help with general administration. Look for ways to share clients with other VAs.

Of course, subcontracting isn't all bad. It's a great way to hone your skills, make some fast (although not good) money, discover the work you like and don't like, and decide how badly you want to work for yourself.

Now that you have created a picture of your ideal client, have practiced your elevator pitch, and have learned that you're not going to become married to your ideas before you share them, it's time to target your clients. Remember, the competition for your ideal client is small. No matter how many VAs are out there, you already know how you're different. While other virtual assistants are targeting everyone, you are targeting the right ones. You speak their secret language. You know their problems and can empathize with them. Your clients aren't generic or bland, and neither are you.

Targeting Your Ideal Client

Get People Excited to Be Your Ideal Client

Probably the most overlooked piece of the ideal client puzzle is how it makes your client feel. Who doesn't want to hear they're ideal? Who wouldn't want to be told that you created your business to serve people just like them? If a company told you those things, how would it make you feel? How would it change your business interactions?

Figure out how to position yourself to be both seen and heard. You need to speak your client's language. Be so specific that the client's name is on the can. Coca-Cola's world famous "Share a Coke" campaign started out by doing just that. When the head of Coca-Cola's South Pacific market saw her name on a can, she said her reaction was "childlike." This campaign became one of the most successful in the company's history.

Forget buzz words. When targeting your client, you want to be so specific that you can call them by name. If you ever forget how to reach them, this is it. If you ever forget how powerful it is to put someone else's name over yours, remember Coke—one of the most iconic logos did and it sparked an international phenomenon.

It's called targeting because you are aiming for something specific, yet most VAs forget to aim at the target. Instead, they talk to everyone but the one they really should be talking to. And they don't get specific enough. Remember to think of it in terms of calling out your client by name. If you shout out "Mom!" in a crowded room, all of the moms will turn their heads. But if you shout out "Melissa!" a smaller group of people will turn their heads. Everyone else is just curious, not a client yet.

Earlier I mentioned Jeffrey Shaw, author of *LINGO*. I like how he describes targeting your ideal client: "You can't unsee a secret language." As Jeffrey explains, part of your ideal client's secret language is the psychology of their behavior. Empathy plays a big part and empathy takes many forms.

As a photographer, holiday greeting cards were part of the lifestyle for Jeffrey's clients. These weren't boxed cards from a store. No, these were cards with photos he had taken and printed on personal stationery, complete with the family's appropriate holiday greeting and complementary color. He even printed their return address on the envelopes! At this point, Jeffrey could have been done. He had delivered a luxury holiday card that more than thrilled his clients. However, empathy spoke words that conveyed the untold secret.

Along with the cards, Jeffrey provided the perfect pen to address the cards, which coordinated with the color of the font in the return address. A note attached to the pen said, "So you don't have to run around town looking for the perfect pen." This reminded his clients he knew that not any pen would do, and he had thought of that too.

How will you empathize with your ideal client? Jeffrey says you can better uncover your clients' surface problems by empathizing with them. You are likely to have been where they are, and you want to prevent them from encountering the same problem again in the future. He also warns about going too deep as it will likely cause you to miss what's right in front of you.

Don't Criticize. Compliment.

You've heard the expression "You can catch more flies with honey than with vinegar." Well, you get more clients by complimenting not criticizing.

Targeting your client, even when they're ideal, can be intimidating. You're going after them, and eventually you'll ask for money, right? If you think of it like this, it *will* be very scary. It's like becoming friends with someone because they have a truck and will be able to help you move the day after you meet. Too soon!

Seems like a no-brainer not to do this with your potential clients, doesn't it? But it happens all the time. A proofreader who publicly points out when someone has errors in their document or social media post. The graphic designer who tells someone what's wrong with their online graphics. The social media specialist who points out all of the missed opportunities.

You don't get clients by criticizing them. There is a way to speak to potential clients. However, you have to earn the right first. The person has to know, like, and trust you. I know this scenario all too well.

I don't have the type of hair that allows me to just wash and go. It's a hot mess at times. While traveling the world, I didn't feel comfortable getting my hair cut just anywhere. Especially a place with language barriers.

I had a very pleasant visit to a salon in Morocco in April 2017. The waxing service was everything I thought it would be, and I was pleased. Then on the way out, it all went bad.

The woman behind the counter had already collected my money, and I was searching for a tip. She looked at me and said, "Wow! You should really let us do something about your hair." I was immediately upset. The first thing that came to my mind was to give her a lesson in customer service. The second thing was to be rude back. What actually came out of my mouth was, "I already have an appointment scheduled." She would have known this if she took the time to ask in a polite way. It was also a missed opportunity.

I would have willingly bought just about any hair product that would make my hair shinier or more manageable. I was open to a treatment, but nothing of the sort was offered. Everything about the conversation was wrong.

You begin to form genuine relationships the moment you engage with your ideal clients. The keyword is "genuine." The reason it's genuine is because you should already know some of the commonalities you share, like books, social groups, associations, causes, favorite places to shop, etc. There's not a chance you're going to come across as fake because, well, you're not.

Complimenting your ideal clients on their work might seem like a fake tactic. You might even think everyone has complimented them already. You'd be wrong. In the age of information overload, when someone shares a piece of their work and the reader takes the time to respond, they receive a positive response in return. Don't believe me? Go to your bookshelf (or Kindle). Turn to the back page of your favorite business book and find the author's information. You'll most commonly find an email address and/or a Twitter handle. Now send an email or a Tweet about why this is your favorite book and explain something that had a great impact on you. It may take a week, but I promise you'll get a response. (In fact, if you are enjoying what you're reading right now, email me at Melissa@thepva.com or send a Tweet to @thepva. I'll respond much faster than a week!)

It works the same with potential clients. Comment on their posts, ask thoughtful questions, join their launch teams, support their endeavors, participate in their surveys. In short, get on their radar. This isn't just to become a fan or a follower. You are learning more about your potential clients. There might be opportunities to leverage their networks and learn even more about what they really need and want. You are eliminating the guessing game.

So what should you do to get clients now? Ask those with whom you already have a relationship. I can almost guarantee you already know your first client. We overlook this area of business because we feel like we're selling to our family and friends in some kind of a pyramid scheme. If you can't ask your family and friends for business referrals, you'll never be able to ask anyone. The excuse of "Well, my family and friends don't need me" is not going to cut it. Asking your family and friends for referrals is a fabulous way to practice fielding questions.

I'll never forget the first time I explained my business to someone (to whom I later found out was the CEO of a large company), and the person immediately understood it. I was at a café in Atlanta where we casually struck up a conversation. I had just finished a phone call, and he asked what I did for a living. I told him I match clients with the right virtual assistants. He went on to ask me a series of questions regarding my business model, which led to my business plan, which then allowed me to tell him about my long-term plans of revenue generation. When we finished, he told me, "Well, looks like you have it all figured out." It wasn't until that moment I was certain I did.

You see, I was constantly talking to everyone about my business, and I somehow always got to a point where someone asked me a question I didn't have the answer to. I should have but I didn't. When I found the answer to that question, inevitably someone new threw me another curveball question. On this day, I hit the curveball out of the park!

When you speak with your family, friends, and colleagues about your business, they'll have questions for you too. It's better to find the answers now rather than when your client asks you the same questions. Practice saying what you offer, who your ideal client is, what value you provide, and how much you charge. No matter how clearly you *think* you speak about your business, someone will always have questions. And questions are a good thing.

Don't get frustrated if someone doesn't understand your business. This is an opportunity for you to refine your focus. This is how you know if what you're saying, offering, and charging attract the same ideal client. If it doesn't, there is a disconnect somewhere and you need to find it.

Begin researching your ideal clients' websites and social media profiles. What do you find in common? Do their photos reveal the same mannerisms? Look at their verbiage. What can you incorporate that you aren't using now? What pains do they speak of to their own clients? These are clues you can use in your own business's tone and messages. We are attracted to people like ourselves and naturally gravitate to the familiar. Become familiar with your potential clients so you seem like the natural choice—the VA who knows them by name.

What Not to Do

There are some things you might be tempted to say to your ideal client because they feel right and on target. They aren't.

- **I work for small business owners.** In the United States, there are 28 million small business owners. Most of those have fewer than 200 employees. When I tell VAs this, they are unaware. You can't target 28 million clients. Your clients aren't in small business—they are in coaching, consulting, insurance, event planning, education, etc. Speak directly to them.

- **Don't promise to save time or money.** Even though both are true, your clients aren't thinking in these terms, nor do you want them to. Time is far too generic. Instead, focus on what they wish they could do with their time. Is it create a course, create a lead magnet with their eBook, manage a project, book more speaking engagements? If you focus on money, they'll focus on how much your rate is. You provide a valuable service, so tell them the value. What is the return on their investment?

When Your Ideal Client Finds You First

When I was meeting and networking with potential clients, I seemed to be attracting a lot of potential clients who weren't a good fit for me. However, I was able to match them with the right virtual assistant. I remember thinking, "Why am I attracting everyone else's potential client? At an event where my ideal client was present, how am I meeting other people's clients?" It turns out I *was* meeting my clients. I was attracting people because I was naturally doing the things I loved—assessing the situation, educating, and then assisting. It just didn't look like it did when I worked in an office.

Your secret language is actually a common language shared between you and your ideal client. Over time the medium may have changed but the message remains the same. Jeffrey Shaw says the best way to find this common language you share is by asking self-identifying questions. "Finish the question in your client's head."

My years as an executive assistant prepared me for this. I worked in education for a long time and was a member of hiring boards. Every time I began a new position, I first had to assess the situation because it was usually at crunch time—no time to ease into my new role. After that, I found where to assist others in making the greatest impact. I couldn't do everything. I found out how to do what mattered and enlist the help of the others for the rest. I'll share a secret with you—I'm super low-tech. With no interest in becoming tech savvy, I found the person who enjoyed tech and swapped tasks. The reason I was on the hiring boards is because I had the knack for knowing when someone was a good fit and when I didn't think they would last the year.

When I finally discovered this, suddenly I realized my potential clients were everywhere. A light bulb went off in my head, and I thought, "Would someone pay me to match them with the right virtual assistant?" I had been matching people for more than a year, and it never occurred to me that someone would pay me for this service!

If you find this is happening to you, it's a sign and you should take notes:

- Who are you attracting? Write down the fields of those whom you "just happen" to keep running into.

- What work are you continuously turning down because you don't have the skill set? You might not have it now, but you could easily learn it. Or like me, you might not have the skills, but you can incorporate one of your current services and now get paid for it.

- What are you providing that is drawing people to you? There is a reason. While you are simply being you, it's exactly the quality that in fact sets you apart from your competitors. You can monetize the quality if you know what it is.

Taking all of these things into consideration, begin looking for the connections—the unasked question and the already presumed answer. What is the quality the world sees in you that you have taken for granted? Look for themes.

This is the part of working with clients that is not linear. Like a scientist conducting experiments, sometimes it's the "accident" that finds the cure. You have to start with the foundation, the problem to solve, and the preliminary actions steps. But after that, be open to experimenting.

In some cases, you might want to consider an internship. Internships are a great way to begin working with clients, especially if your ideal client is in a field that's foreign to your own experiences. Internships present amazing learning opportunities if done right.

I'm very particular about the type of internships I endorse. In fact, I have VAs contact me on a regular basis to be my intern. I have yet to have an intern because I believe in getting paid, and I believe in paying people. No one has asked to learn from me. They offered services—services I could not mentor them on. That would not have been the right type of internship, and I declined. I'll share with you how to do an internship properly in the bonus chapter.

Summary

- Now you know about the importance of networking and the different types of networking available to you. Most importantly, networking is only effective when it's done at the right places and with a specific plan. Don't forget to take networking offline whenever possible. Look for a networking partner and create a game plan.

- Carefully determine which groups—both online and in person— you are going to invest your time and money networking in. Knowing the purpose for the group you're joining is essential to get the most out of it.

- You know how to create an elevator pitch that is concise and repeatable. Practice it often to refine it and get feedback from your ideal clients.

- We've discussed how to follow up after networking and how to ask for referrals the right way.

- You know how to get people excited to be your ideal client and how to use empathy when speaking your client's secret language. You also know how to get on the radar of your clients and support them before they become your clients. Plus, you know what not to do.

- I've shared what it looks like when your ideal client finds you first and how this is a great business opportunity.

We've covered a lot in this chapter because it all goes hand in hand. You shouldn't be networking without knowing who you are networking with and why. Additionally, your words should always speak to your ideal client. Ideally, you are always in the right place, whether you're networking for support or to gain clients.

In the next chapter, we'll discuss one of the most sensitive topics, managing yourself and the client relationship. Without knowing how to successfully navigate this process, you cannot grow or sustain your business. It's also how you avoid burnout.

CHAPTER 6

Step 6: Managing Yourself and the Client Relationship

This is one of the most important chapters in the book. This is where elite VAs separate themselves from the rest. I'm going to be giving you a lot of straight talk information here. It won't be easy to do it, but the payoff will be worth it.

This is the point in many VA businesses where VAs didn't plan for success, growth, and having difficult conversations. They never learn how to get to the other side and subsequently decide it's too difficult, leaving them short of accomplishing their goals and dreams. Worse, some quit after working so hard in the beginning. Burnout, frustration, and being shackled to the business in the worst way possible, they believe it would be better to become an employee again.

Managing your business is different than managing your workload. Working for yourself comes with having to set entirely new boundaries. Boundaries that couldn't have been legally crossed when you were an employee. One of the most common reasons I see virtual assistants burn themselves out is because no boundaries were set from the beginning, and suddenly their work and personal lives become so chaotic they have to shut down business to save their personal lives.

I don't believe in the term "work-life balance." Balancing gives equal attention to different things in your life. Not everything in your life requires the same amount of attention at exactly the same time. When something unexpected occurs—and it will—your balance is thrown off. I do believe in "work-life integration." Folding all the areas of your life into everyday life and providing attention to the things and people who need and deserve it at the right time will keep you sane. You'll know that whatever you're giving your attention to is the right thing.

Set Boundaries

Boundaries. Boundaries. Boundaries.

If the three most important things in real estate are location, location, and location, then the three most important things in your business are boundaries, boundaries, and boundaries. Both in life and in business, people will only treat you the way you allow them to. How long does it take for a client to cross a boundary? It can happen almost immediately. The problem comes when you don't let them know they've crossed a boundary. From then on, things will never be the same.

So often we think when a client wants to cross our boundaries, it is cause for conflict, confrontation, or concern. It is none of those things. If someone is crossing a boundary, it's because they don't know it's there. We all do it. It's our natural tendency to want and ask for more. If someone takes more and then gets it, they'll keep going back until they're told not to. If a client asks for more and you give it, the client will keep expecting it. They didn't cross a boundary since they asked. You didn't have a boundary to begin with, and now changing things will be extremely difficult.

Nothing is better than taking care of the situation the first time it occurs. You'll never get this opportunity back. Here's how a typical scenario goes:

The client asks you to do something you don't normally do. Out of the kindness of your heart, you agree to complete the task. The client continues to ask you for this work, and you continue to do it. A few weeks or months down the road, you go to the client and make your case. You either let them know you can't do this task anymore because it wasn't what you originally agreed upon, or you offer to continue doing the task but you'll have to charge XYZ. Either way, the client is not happy and you are ultimately at fault.

Another common scenario is the client keeps adding to your workload, giving you last-minute projects with quick deadlines, including emails and text messages at all hours of the day and night. You don't schedule a meeting to discuss setting priorities and instead try to juggle all of the projects. You work to complete the last-minute tasks, but inevitably you make errors because that's what happens when things are done in a rush. You answer every email and text the moment it comes in. Then one day, you realize how miserable you are. And because you don't like confrontation, you decide it's easier to quit. You've just created a non-believer in the world of VAs. You have nothing to show for your time in the form of a referral, and you might even be a little bitter. This is when the client "cleansing" starts to happen.

Both of these scenarios play out daily for VAs around the world. And these situations are the most common amongst new VAs. You are so used to having to do everything for your employer that you forget you no longer have one. You don't get to go home from the office anymore to escape—you're already home.

In both of these scenarios, being the owner of your business, you could have redirected these conversations using your boundaries. Boundaries with your clients aren't meant to be a fortress to keep them out. These are not castle walls with a moat and alligators. When you think of your boundaries, think of how they might be viewed to your clients—a white picket fence, a front door that's never locked, a gate with a special code. How does your client get to you?

When you think of it like this, your perspective will change. I have an open door policy. My clients don't keep regular business hours, nor do I. Their clients pay them a premium price, and my clients pay me a premium price. We also respect one another. When they contact me at odd times, I know it's urgent. We're both too busy to waste anyone's time.

When you're tasked with something you don't do or didn't include in your original contract, it's as easy as telling the client. Ask the client if he or she would like a proposal that outlines the cost to add the task to your current agreement. Or offer to find a VA who does perform this service.

So many VAs say nothing in this scenario because they are afraid of saying no. So don't say no. Instead, offer other options. Don't tell clients what they can't have; give options so they can decide what is right for them.

Imagine you're at a restaurant. The server seems nice and pleasant. As she takes your order, you ask to make a substitution. Her response is "No." Then she walks away. This would not go over well. What normally happens is what plays out in business too. She tells you, "Sure, but it will cost extra." And she tells you exactly how much. Either you happily agree, change your order, or decline the substitution. If she's a good server, she'll help you get to your decision faster by finding a way to get you what you want, even if it's done creatively. If one of your dining companions doesn't want the salad that comes with the meal, the server offers it to you, and it won't cost you a dime.

In the second scenario, you are the person who is feeding the squirrels and then wondering how to get rid of them. In the beginning, the workload is likely to increase before it gets to a maintenance level. Last minute tasks will frequently come up because the client will continuously think of new things to give you. They're excited! What they need from you is help managing it all. Where VAs go wrong is trying to do it all. It can't be done without a plan. You can manage a plan. You can't manage a task, only perform it.

Your client doesn't have to be a part of your management system. They do need to be a part of your thought process. First things first, when you get the communication coming in (we've already established this is the preferred method for both of you), they should know what you're doing with it. Do you check emails once a day or at certain times during the day, or do you promise to respond within 24 hours? Personally, I find it easiest to read and respond to emails while the client is online. Otherwise, I respond with "Received." This lets the client know that I got the message, and it puts the client at ease. They don't have to wonder if the message got lost in cyberspace or if it went to your spam folder.

The second part of the conversation is to let the client know your workflow. Does one thing play off the other? Is what they sent you time sensitive? Are the projects conflicting? Don't ever assume and don't ever make the decision for them. Recap a previous conversation about workflow, explain in detail what the new workflow and timeline will look like, and ask if they are in agreement. If not, call the client. Don't go back and forth over email. A two-minute phone call will end in smiles. Six back and forth e-mails will leave them wondering why they hired you when they could've done the work already.

Pick your battles and always do the right thing. Don't argue and don't make the point of being right. Be the friendly voice and the friendly email on the other side. You know—the person you were during the consultation.

Clients aren't the only offenders of boundaries. You will likely break your own rules. They don't seem as hard on you, but you will still take them out on your client if you're not careful. Your business or projects can't tell you when you've crossed your own boundaries. Just stay aware.

Here are several ways to set boundaries for yourself that are easy to keep:

- **Create natural breaks.** Take a break for meals—real meals that you eat off plates at a table, not eating a quick bite at your computer. Step away from your desk or workspace. Even better, share a meal with someone.

- **Have a dedicated time to start and stop your day.** Don't work just because you can. Additionally, if you know that you have to stop at a certain time, you will finish what you need to accomplish faster. It's Parkinson's law: "Work expands to fill the time available for its completion."

- **Schedule events to look forward to.** When you look forward to a specific event, it will excite you throughout the week. You can work off of that great energy, and it helps you stick to your stop times. (Another reason I plan so many days off!)

- **Pick two days of the week that you don't work.** It doesn't have to be a traditional weekend schedule, but choose two days that fit your schedule best. If you don't do this now, when your business explodes you won't know how to take time off to enjoy your own success. Family and friend commitments will soon become obsolete because you'll always be too busy. If you want to take a vacation or a long weekend, you won't know how. If you lose a day or two to being sick, you'll be completely behind.

- **Get help before you need it.** An ounce of prevention is worth a pound of cure, right? Having an urgent need can confuse your judgment or cause you to act fast without weighing all the options. Having the help you need before you need it is priceless.

Many virtual assistants know how to get others organized yet allow our own businesses to become disorganized. We're like the cobbler's kids who have no shoes. It's not our clients' job to be productive. It's ours. So are you? What does your inbox look like? Who is waiting on you? Which projects need your attention?

I've found the very thing you assist clients with is also the task that holds you back. My clients struggle with working all the time. I struggle with working all the time too. Remember when I said our avatars mirror ourselves? It's true in the not so good habits as well. While it's great to be able to understand our clients and their needs, it's also something you should be looking out for.

One of the most common reasons we don't realize it's happening is because it means business is booming. Our efforts are paying off, and we're more than willing to work longer hours, including nights and weekends. The adrenaline has kicked in, and we want to capitalize on everything coming our way to keep the momentum going. The problem is we don't work in a bubble with no outside commitments. We have lives outside of work too.

Whatever type of VA you are, you must have a system for working with your clients. You might even set up systems for their work, but never overlook setting up systems for your own business—a system that runs efficiently and ensures nothing falls through the cracks in the process. As a virtual assistant I know you know this. Yet, when your business grows, your systems don't seem to grow fast enough. You won't learn about the cracks until it's too late.

There are some instances where a crack in the system is an opportunity for you to rethink your business. If one client keeps you up at night versus the others whom you work with seamlessly, is this client your ideal? What type of services are you offering to this client that you aren't offering the others? Do you need to rethink your clients, your prices, or your processes?

Is Doing What You Love Killing You?

I'm almost an adrenaline junkie. I don't get my adrenaline high by jumping out of airplanes or off cliffs. The closest I came was jumping on the back of a scooter with a complete stranger in Hanoi after randomly yelling out, "Motorbike!" I was rewarded with a tour around the city. Riding a scooter, even as a passenger, in Hanoi is quite an experience. Oncoming traffic, more traffic than you've ever seen in your life, driving so close to everyone that you're swapping skin and paint, no rules, and add in the fact that I had no idea where I was going or what I was doing. It all made for quite an adrenaline rush.

Sometimes I can run my business the same way. My business coach once looked me straight in the eyes and told me I was "addicted." If I didn't find a way to survive without my work, it would be a slow death.

I didn't know what he was talking about, and I almost resented him for saying it. The previous few weeks in my business had been great! I signed a big contract with an amazing new client, and I sent out another contract of the same amount for another client I was excited to work for as well. My Admin to VA Summit went live. I was booked with podcast interviews, consulting, and writing. It's everything I had ever wanted. And oh yeah, I was traveling the world!

In this situation, the first thing most people usually suggest is delegating tasks to others. That isn't my problem. I take my own advice and have virtual assistants for a variety of different tasks. My problem is that I add work into any time I gain. I see open time on my schedule as an opportunity to do more. Earn more. Grow faster.

Does any of this sound familiar? Don't allow the love of what you do and the potential of growing your business to kill your business or take you to the point of exhaustion. If you are addicted to work like me, sometimes you'll have to take drastic measures to reduce your workload. For me, it's taking a vacation at a moment's notice. I'm best at disconnecting when I'm on vacation. That's the drastic part. You must disconnect and get away from things.

It blows my mind when people wonder how some people can work virtually. Not only can you work from anywhere in the world, you can also overwork from anywhere in the world. I'm possibly one of the worst offenders. No one ever tells me to work harder or stop procrastinating. They tell me to slow down and take time to rest—something you might think is easy since I'm hanging out in some pretty great locations. But it's still hard for me to stop and rest.

Wherever you are, love yourself more than you love what you do. Not everyone will understand what I'm saying. Great for them! I'm trying to get to the place they already are. For the rest of us, work will always be here. We won't ever get back to this time and place.

Did You Burn Yourself Out?

Do you still have warm fuzzies about your virtual assistant business? Are you excited to get up in the morning and work with your clients? You know, the ones you tried so desperately to get when you first started. The clients you didn't know were out there. Before you realized you could make it on your own. You should be.

Business ownership can be a dream. However, for too many, it's become a nightmare. We, as virtual assistants, have pulled our clients' business lives together so they can have time for their personal lives, which so closely overlap. Yet when it comes to our own businesses, we drop the ball in this area.

We forget about creating automation and planning strategy sessions. We work too much. We don't make plans for the weeks and months down the road. We don't pay attention to the upcoming workflow or the sales pipeline. It's time to show your business some love again.

First, automate you. Don't ask for another you. That will only create more work for yourself. Do whatever you need to do to so things function automatically. This could mean hiring your own VA. Don't skimp on this task. If you don't have the time now, you won't have the time later. Plus, if you wait until you need to do it, then it's too late.

Work a four-day week. You can certainly be available to your clients five days a week but make plans to get the work done in four. Should something come up during this time that puts you behind, now you'll have an extra day instead of possibly working late or on one of your scheduled days off.

Have a three-week to three-month strategy. Begin planning your time out in three-week blocks, whether or not your clients give you work that far in advance. Be proactive and anticipate your clients' needs before they ask you for help. As you master a three-week time period, keep moving forward until you can plan three months in advance.

Again, it is your job to be proactive with your clients. Last minute items you keep completing at the last minute will always be requested at the last minute. You're not providing a service to your clients; you're enabling them. Think of the stress they're under to be constantly working against the clock. Help your clients make the change. They'll thank you for it.

Now plan. Plan vacations. Plan to attend conferences. Plan to learn a new skill. Don't wait until you have time. Make time. These are the things you wanted to do when you began your business. Remember how you dreamed of what you would do when you weren't chained to a desk and had someone looking over your shoulder? Remember when you had downtime at work and wanted to go to a yoga class, play with your children, read a book, or run errands? Do those things now! Well, running errands isn't super exciting, but if you time it right—while everyone else is at work!—it can take you half the time.

Do the things you need to do to love your VA business again. It doesn't happen by accident, and it doesn't happen overnight. Imagine what you want it to be and make it so. Love yourself and your business enough to wake up excited every day to do your work. This is the life you gave yourself. You became a VA business owner. Love it or leave it!

Why Vacations Are So Important

While traveling the world in 2017, I took a record number of vacation days. I had a lot of people wonder why it's necessary for me to take a vacation while I'm traveling the world. For starters, just because I was traveling the world didn't mean I wasn't working. Whenever you're working, you need to take time off. No matter how excited I was to travel to the next country, I was aware that my mind and body needed to disconnect.

Additionally, launching three new products in a single year meant I was putting in a lot more hours. Business was booming, and all my launches had to be created during the same time I was matchmaking, assisting, and consulting with clients. More work time made it a must for me to take more vacation time. Here's a tip: Anytime you're working so hard you feel like you don't have time for something is when you need it the most.

If you work from home or a remote location as a virtual assistant, people may not realize you're really working. They cling to an old-fashioned mentality of taking a vacation from the office and the commute, which is still true for many. Since 55 percent of Americans had unused vacation days last year, you can bet taking time off when you're already working virtually seems odd. I encourage you to be the odd one!

Average and successful are not synonymous. You'll have to choose who you want to be. I'll give you three reasons to take a vacation before you think you are successful enough to do so:

1. Taking a vacation gives you a successful mindset.

My vacations didn't always include international travel. In previous years, most of them included staying with family to save on hotel costs. When I first started my business, it often seemed counterintuitive to take a vacation. On paper, I wasn't making enough money to take time off. Everything I read told me to suffer through the first two years and make sacrifices. However, it didn't seem right. Turned out I was reading the wrong things.

I told my own clients to take vacations, but I refused to follow my own advice. How hypocritical! I couldn't tell someone to do something I was not doing myself. Benjamin Hardy wrote an article called "The 2 Mental Shifts Highly Successful People Make." The first shift is The Power of Choice. He writes, "The foundation of the first shift is the sublime power of choice and individual responsibility. Once you make this shift, you are empowered to pull yourself from poverty of time, finances, and relationships. In other words, the first shift allows you to create a happy and prosperous life, where, for the most part, you control how and on what you invest your time." Not taking a vacation is a choice. You are choosing to tell yourself you are not worthy of a much-needed break. If you keep telling yourself this, you won't ever escape from the poverty of that thinking. Instead, it will become true.

If you're not making enough money yet (*YET!*) to take the vacation of your dreams, I understand. Save, plan, and *still* take a vacation this year. You don't have to go far away to disconnect. Do a Google search to find every free attraction in a 50-mile radius of your home. Enjoy a picnic or a hike. Read a book or create movie nights. Find out if you have any friends or family leaving town and offer to house-sit so you can be in different surroundings. Vacation isn't merely a destination. It's a mindset, a choice.

2. Take a summer vacation to be successful in the fall.

In a Forbes article titled "10 Reasons You Cannot Afford Not to Take a Vacation," we learn, "Whereas summer is a quiet period for most companies, autumn is a power session. Together with spring it's the most important sales period . . ." If you were running a race tomorrow, you wouldn't stay out all night tonight. You'd make sure you were well rested so you could do your best. Vacationing in the summer is the same thing. As the article goes on to say, "So rather than thinking of a break as something you do for yourself, then do it for the sake of your company's future productivity."

Many virtual assistants think they can't take a vacation if they don't have a full client load. In fact, vacationing before you have a lot of clients is best. You'll learn how to plan, automate, and manage the time while you're gone. If you aren't able to do this with a few clients, you won't be able to do it with many.

3. Taking a vacation makes you more productive and positions you for success.

Our brains, like our bodies, need a break to perform better. You would never train for a marathon by running 26.2 miles every day. Your body would not have time to recover, and you could not avoid injuries, which cause major setbacks. Well, you might not feel mental fatigue as quickly as you experience physical fatigue, but it's there and it happens sooner. "Since almost all of us are doing mental work these days, managing cognitive resources is not a nice thing to be able to do; it's essential," according to the article "The Secret to Increased Productivity: Taking Time Off" in *Entrepreneur*. As virtual assistants, it is extremely important that we take vacations. When we don't, we're not taking our own advice.

If your business isn't set up to run without you, you're not creating anything sustainable, and you can forget about being scalable. Vacation isn't something you wait to do until be you become successful. It's what you do because you're already thinking like a successful business owner.

Being successful is a mindset. If you don't think you're successful enough to take a vacation, you probably won't ever be.

This isn't fake it until you make it. I'm telling you to put good and best practices in place now so you can build and grow from a solid foundation. In life and in business, you can't help or serve anyone if you aren't already helping and serving yourself.

Are You in a Funk? Give Yourself a Hard Reset.

I vividly remember the last words my son said on New Year's Eve 2016. As I rolled my luggage toward the Bay Area Rapid Transit (BART) station, fighting to hold back tears, preparing to travel the world (12 countries in 12 months), not knowing if I would see him the entire year, he yelled out to me, "Kick 2017's ass, Mom!"

While many people assumed I was taking a year off from work, or at least taking it very easy, those closest to me knew better. In 2017 I made some big plans, and since I work virtually, I can do them from anywhere in the world. Not only was I going on this yearlong journey for myself, I was on a mission to show how much can be done while working remotely—even if you are traveling the world.

By August 2017, I had already proved a lot. If you want to know what I accomplished in the first six months of the year, you can read my article "Want to Challenge How Much Work Can Be Done Remotely?" I purposely front-loaded the majority of my work for the year, knowing most of the long working days would be behind me by this time so I could start writing my next book. The plan I put in place had been executed. Then something unexpected happened—I got into this weird "funk."

At a point in the year when I assumed the easiest work was ahead of me, I started to shut down. I say it's the easiest because I love writing, and the majority of the book had already been written. I did everything I could to shake the funk, and nothing helped.

I was trying to pinpoint the exact thing that was causing me to hold myself back, but I couldn't. It wasn't just one thing. It was a multitude of things. Eight months into the year and two product launches later, dealing with the unexpected ups and downs of life had caught up with me.

Until now I had adapted to the situation or powered through. It's what we do as virtual assistants, business owners, and entrepreneurs. The problem was I had adapted so much that I got away from myself. Powering through works until you have no more steam. Worse, since I was no longer working like I do when I do have steam, I didn't really know what to do with this unexpected funk. It was time to give myself a hard reset.

A hard reset meant restoring myself to "original factory settings." It meant no longer adapting to anything or anyone, rather doing it my way. I had to look back at the last year to remember when I was my best and what that looks like for me.

The hard reset was about getting back to me—my schedule, my priorities, my work, and my play. Only then would I have control over the thing I can actually control—myself. I was in a funk because I wasn't controlling the one thing I could. And worse, I was allowing other things to control me while being overly adapted to an environment in which I wouldn't live for more than a month.

My hard reset included:

- Waking up at 5 a.m. every day.

- Running three to five times a week.

- Reading every night before I go to bed.

- Every night writing down my three must-dos for the next day.

- Eating healthy foods and getting plenty of sleep.

I have complete control over all of these things. Doing them is what it took to get back to me. When I do these things, I am much better prepared to handle all the situations I cannot control on a daily basis. As virtual assistants, we are natural givers. Sometimes we give until it hurts us, literally. You can't serve or assist anyone when you're not at your best.

You may not have planned any product launches this year, and you may not be traveling extensively. However, there will be times when you find yourself adapting to your current situation. New firsts, new beginnings, new endings, and a host of other situations you've needed to adapt to.

During these times, I cannot stress enough the need to take care of yourself. When you don't, you will begin to question your work, your clients, and your value. If you cannot manage yourself first, you will not be able to manage your client relationships.

Managing the Client

Everything in your business needs to be managed, including your clients. If you don't manage them, they will manage you. You're already on the right track if you set boundaries for yourself. The next part of managing the client is acting like and speaking like a business owner.

It comes from every action, every response, every experience, and every form of communication. Once you break one of these, you confuse the client. I can't imagine walking into Tiffany & Co. without someone opening the door for me. That might be strange. Could you imagine if I left the store with a purchase, and it wasn't wrapped in their famous blue box? I would demand one. They are managing their customer relationships every step of the way. The beauty of it is that it's all for my benefit.

The first step in managing the client relationship is in your onboarding process, which begins during the consultation. Onboarding requires effort on your part, especially proper communication. Most VAs get it wrong when they are trying to get the client to work for them. Instead, you should be creating expectations for your client. The difference is in how the client feels about the onboarding process. Sending a packet for your new client to read is not onboarding; that is homework. They hired you to have less work to do, and you're giving them work before the real work even begins!

During your consultation appointment, you should have uncovered your client's working style. This will give you insights into how your onboarding process should work. In the simplest of terms, onboarding is setting the expectations of how you'll be working together, how you'll be communicating, what work will be getting done, and the time frames to complete the work.

When clients know what to expect, onboarding becomes a less scary process. When they don't know what to expect, you are surprising them in the wrong way. Don't assume the same excitement they had during your consultation still exists. In the 24 hours after your consultation appointment, they could already be experiencing buyer's remorse. Be ready to answer more questions now if need be. Having a time line will help answer these questions each time you gain a new client.

First, your clients must know they have been heard. Based on what they've shared with you, you've created a time line for your working relationship. This could be a new experience for the client.

I use the same time line for all of my potential clients because the schedule for fulfilling their needs is always the same. This is not rocket science for me. For them it could be as frightening as getting in a rocket to the moon. They are handing over money and trusting I am going to do what I said I would do. Is there excitement? Yes. Are they scared? Yes. It's more than working with me. Now they are going to have additional expenses. They are going to have to work differently. It's scary and exciting to grow a business. When you onboard a client, it is to put him or her at ease.

After sharing a project time line, next you must make sure you have a communication strategy time line. This puts you at ease. Don't wait until you need something. Your client is busy, which is why he or she hired you. If you aren't scheduled on your client's calendar now, a time will come when you will need to speak to him or her the most, and there simply won't be enough time on the client's calendar. Suddenly, your project time line will start to diminish.

Communicate but don't overshare. You destroy the boundaries and break your own rules about your time when you overshare what you're doing. No one needs to know when you have a doctor's appointment. It's no one's business if you're sitting in a café reading a book or at a yoga class in the middle of the day. You're not exchanging your time for money. You're exchanging services for money. If you are professional, simply provide a quality service in a timely manner and that's all your clients need to know.

The only exception is when it's time to vacation. Notify your clients well in advance and make sure things are taken care of.

Honesty may be the best policy, but timing is your best friend. My daughter has impeccable timing. She knows where I'm at mentally before she asks for money, and when she asks for it, I'm almost excited to transfer it. My son, on the other hand, is not always so fortunate, and instead of making a quick transfer, I find myself giving a lengthy lecture. There are times you will be candid and honest with your client when something didn't go well. But anytime is not the right time. Choose a time when your client will be the most receptive to your conversation.

How you share is equally important. If you incorrectly scheduled an email sequence, you don't have time to text or email the client and say something vague like, "We have an issue" or "There was an error in that last email." Panic, anger, or frustration set in quickly, and you'd better hope they aren't in a situation where they can't contact you for several hours. That's a pot rising to a rolling boil.

What do you do? Send a message with a brief explanation of what happened. State that you are aware, and you are fixing it. Make yourself available if the client wants to speak now or later. Don't send an email and then say you're not available because you're taking your kids to practice. What time do you think it is for your client?

Managing your client relationship is also about managing your client time line. A client's launch is your launch. If you are not available during the launch, it's a mistake. At the very least, your client should know well in advance that you are unavailable, and you should have created an SOP (standard operating procedures) guide to be ready to handle anything they need to on the backend in your absence.

When it comes to managing your first big time client, you will have jitters. You may question yourself and your abilities. You know you can do it, and the client does too. But right now you keep questioning yourself. This is leveling up again. Fear and excitement come with the territory. Remind yourself why the client hired you. This is important because often when VAs get their first big client or level up to a new clientele base, they allow the clients to set the expectations and the way they work. Big mistake.

Allowing the client to run the order and workflow is the tail wagging the dog. There is a lot clients run. They can't also run the very thing they hired you to do. You can't own work, systems, and procedures you didn't create. And you know what will happen if it all goes bad—they'll blame you. The argument of "I was following instructions" will mean little. If you knew they were doing it wrong and you didn't say anything, that is even worse. They just paid you to create a mess of their business.

Which brings up another question. Who pays for the mistakes? You do. If a restaurant gets your order wrong, if the drycleaner loses your dress, if the valet wrecks your car, you wouldn't expect to pay for any of those things. Why would your client pay extra to fix what you broke? If it's something that naturally might need to be revised, revision pricing should have been included in the original pricing. Nickel and diming is for the other guys. We provide an excellent service, put in the hours, and are compensated appropriately. Besides, what could you even buy for a nickel?

Educating Your Clients Effectively

Educating clients can be tricky. How much information do you give? How much do you charge? How long should you spend sharing information with them? How do you present it to them? These are common questions virtual assistants ask in online forums.

Often we know what our clients don't. That's why they hire us. However, the key element here is that we are speaking about *clients*. Not prospective clients. Not people we've had consultations with. Clients are the business owners who have already paid us, and yet they still have questions that need to be answered. Why does your client still have so many questions? Trust.

In Matthew Harrington's Harvard Business Review article "Survey: People's Trust Has Declined in Business, Media, Government, and NGOs," he sheds much-needed light on what is happening in our society. As your clients' VA, you can't assume giving you money means they trust you. Paying people and companies is part of life. Trust is earned. It is your job to build it, earn it, and hold on to it.

Creating trust with your clients isn't just for yourself. It's also for the benefit of virtual assistants everywhere. Do you know why clients have so little trust? Often it's because a VA before you did not deliver how she said she would and could. The business owner is now taking a leap of faith again to hire you. You not only have to prove your worth, you also have to make them forget the other VA.

The most common issue I come across is the virtual assistant a client first hired wasn't a good fit, which is why they hire me to find the right VA. I don't hear questions; I hear the problems. From there, I have to dig deeper to understand what they really mean. What are your clients asking you? Now figure out what they really mean. Most importantly, remove your feelings and put yourself in their shoes.

How much information do you give? Whatever it takes to put them at ease. I will give you a tip—it's much less than you think. Don't send a link. Don't redirect them to your website. Don't just send them a contract. Not only is it rude, but it doesn't address what they're really asking because they don't know until you ask. So ask:

- "What concerns you?"

- "How can I put your mind at ease?"

- "In a perfect world, what would the outcome be?"

- "What are you afraid is going to happen?"

Now you're ready to tackle the real issue. Your responses should first address the clients' concerns and then explain your overall action, what you have in place to meet their needs.

How much do you charge? Nothing. This question actually frustrates me. You can't charge for a phone call, an online chat, an email, or a text. Nothing. You can't charge because 1) the client is already paying you, 2) this was your responsibility to take care of during the consultation, and 3) it would be very unprofessional. We're not lawyers or psychiatrists or any other profession known to charge clients for speaking to them. Can you imagine if your doctor gave you a prescription and then charged you extra to explain how it will help you?

How long do you spend sharing information with them? You never stop sharing. You don't have the luxury to work on an island (no matter how remote you are) and then check in when you feel like it. The client is paying you for your work. Determine your communication strategy, know what they what to know, determine how often they want to know it, and then deliver on it. Sharing only takes a long time and becomes a burden when what you're sharing isn't what the client was asking for.

How do you present it to them? In their preferred format. Anything less and your message will not get through. Again, this goes back to determining the best communication strategy.

If you can't willingly and happily work with a client in this manner, you are not working with your ideal client. Educating your clients is an ongoing process, even after trust is established. It's natural for your clients to ask why. It's a smart business person who asks questions and wants to know the ins and outs of their business. The right way to educate your clients is to build trust. Be sure you're earning trust while you work for them.

Should You Focus on Pleasing People or Serving People?

Managing the client isn't pleasing the client. People-pleasing is a slippery slope. The idea is fantastic. Who doesn't want to please people? If you're an assistant of any kind, it seems like an automatic and necessary part of your job. When people aren't happy, it's your job to fix it, right? Here's when you usually hop on the downward slope.

You aren't in control of anyone's happiness. There are definite times when you are a contributor, but you can't make someone else happy. In the same manner, no one is responsible for pleasing you and making sure you are always happy. However, you can and should serve your clients. To serve someone isn't always to make them happy.

Serving people is much more finite and takes emotions out of the equation. I consider myself a pretty emotional person. One who cries at commercials, sunrises, sunsets, and art. A person who will also laugh until I'm in tears, even at myself. However, having strong emotions in business isn't always positive or logical. It is not uncommon for a person to have strong emotions and not know why. Feelings and emotions change. Facts don't.

When it's my time to serve my client, the goal isn't for the client to reach an emotional high and be pleased. Of course, I want to provide an experience that surpasses the goal, but I'm not in charge of the goal. The client is. Nor can I reach the goal without first providing excellent service. My goal first and foremost must be to serve.

How you serve is as important as the service you provide. They go hand in hand. You have to start at the end and work your way to the beginning. This will let you know what your final work will look like and provide the route to accomplish it in a way so your client feels served.

For instance, if you are working on a project and know your deadline as well as what the end result will look like, the client may or may not be served if she doesn't hear from you in the interim. It doesn't matter if you achieved exactly what the client wanted. If she doesn't feel served you can trust she won't be pleased. You could very well please the client and not serve her a positive end result. A common complaint is a virtual assistant who is very sweet and pleasant, the client likes her, but the service is not good. The service includes your work and how you go about delivering it.

Here's how to set up a service plan, making service the first priority and setting yourself up to be in a position to please the client:

Begin at the end.

I've said it before, and I'll say it again—start with expectations. However, don't just find out what the client's expectations are. Set your own. If you only agree and don't offer any feedback, you are focused on pleasing people not serving them. It's your job to help your clients set realistic expectations or offer advice on a better practice. Let them decide the final outcome based on your expert feedback. Few things are worse than when the person you hired to help you remains silent when he or she has the ability to help make things better.

Know and share your mapped-out route.

Communication strategy is critical. Creating your checkpoints in the beginning gives everyone an overview of how the working relationship will function. If you'll need check-ins and feedback at certain intervals or proofs to be approved, these should be discussed in the beginning. Does the client know what happens if they don't respond in a timely manner? Will this move them back in your queue? Do you have rush job fees? It's all fair and reasonable if the client knows this up front. Clients might prefer a specific day to receive emails or may have their own firm deadlines, such as before a vacation or a conference. A good communication strategy means you will collect all of this information directly from your clients

If you were driving across country and learned there isn't another rest area for 100 miles, you would most certainly share this with your passengers. The same is true for your clients. In these circumstances, surprises don't delight clients.

Be prepared to deliver.

The saddest thing you can do is lose the client in delivery. It's sad because everything you've done up until this point is absolutely worthless now. Every consult, every email, every call is forgotten if you deliver the final piece incorrectly. How will you serve the final product?

You don't think it's important? You think your work will speak for itself? You're wrong. Imagine dining out at a fancy restaurant. You've waited for this night for weeks. You might have even bought a new outfit. The hostess was kind and made sure you got the table you wanted. Upon arrival, you were warmly greeted and promptly seated at the table. The restaurant has the right lighting and music. The view is extraordinary. Then it all goes downhill.

The server spills water on you while carelessly pouring it into your glass. Another server throws some bread on the table. The special entrées are half-heartedly rattled off, and when the sommelier arrives at your table, he treats you like an idiot for not knowing as much about wine as he does.

Wine is poured without offering for you to taste it, since you don't have extensive wine knowledge. When the meal is served, the plates are slammed down and the food looks like it was dumped on the plate. Did the flavor of the bread, wine, or food actually change due to the way it was served? No. Does it leave a bad taste in your mouth? Absolutely. It's all about delivery.

You say it's all about the money, and small projects and tasks don't matter? Think back to the last time you ordered a pizza. When you opened the box, was the cheese on the pizza or on the inside top of the box? Delivery matters.

Don't shy away from difficult conversations.

You could follow all these steps and serve the client. What do you do if the client isn't pleased? You must have a difficult conversation. And do it on the phone, on a video chat, or in person. Take it offline. Back and forth emails or texts will only make a difficult conversation worse.

Here's where you need to uncover the root of the problem and ask questions. Do not ask emotional questions, such as "What aren't you happy with?" or "How can I please you?" Emotional questions invite emotional responses. Instead ask questions like,

- "What didn't meet your expectations?"

- "When you envisioned the final product, what was missing from the actual result?"

- "How can I satisfy your expectations?"

If you have not read *Difficult Conversations* by Douglas Stone, Bruce Patton, and Sheila Heen, you must. No matter how long you've been in business or how many satisfied clients you have, there will come a day when you need to have a difficult conversation. No other book will prepare you like this one.

You won't ever win the people-pleasing game. It's impossible to be all things to all clients. Instead, focus on serving people. Only then can you please them as a byproduct. To be served is what people really want, even if they don't know it. If they didn't want to be served, they wouldn't have hired you in the first place.

VAs don't do damage control. We find the win-win situation. Damage control is for the other guys. We find a way to make the client feel like a winner not a triaged victim. If you're doing damage control, there better have been a natural disaster.

What Type of Experience Do Your Clients Want?

I love to experience things. I seek out new experiences on a regular basis. Other times I go back to have the same experience as I did before. It's a rare company that can duplicate or exceed an experience. You know what I'm talking about—one day your cup of coffee is perfect, but the next day it's too sweet or too bitter.

While I traveled the world, I made it a point to have a true experience in each country. In several countries, the experience I couldn't wait to take part in was a local massage. I had my best experiences in Bogota, Belgrade, and Hanoi. While each experience was genuinely unique, they all incorporated the same basic principles. Some of these principles I already used with my own clients, but for others I was going to figure out a way to include them in the future.

The first step is expectation. Sound familiar? I wasn't left wondering where to go, what to do, or what was going to happen next. I was told all of the details, and I was able to anticipate what was coming. Before each massage, I was either signaled by a sound or told by the masseuse we were about to begin. This seemingly small act made a big difference. Often it was the way the massage ended as well. I wasn't wondering if the time was up or what was going to happen next.

The beginning of your client working relationship should be solid, and the client should not be surprised at what is about to take place. They should expect a contract, an invoice, and an onboarding process, as well as a timeline.

What experience do your clients want? Don't think about what you're providing, but what do they want? Don't guess, ask. It is important to know if you are giving them what they want. Or maybe you're actually giving them more than they want. Far too often we do what we like and assume the client is just as pleased. Don't make those kinds of assumptions. Surprise and delight are far too overrated.

First off, if you are surprising your clients because you are giving them such quality service, somewhere along the way you went wrong. You didn't come off very well in the consultation or the client was leery and now you've put them at ease (think about all the potential clients you didn't win over) or your prices are so low they've gotten the deal of the century. Your services and pricing should be the expectation.

Delighting someone is good, but it doesn't last. You can only keep doing this for so long before it wears off and you have to keep outdoing yourself. Instead, it is better to consistently meet and exceed expectations and goals, then celebrate your victories.

You want to be as predictable as the sun rising in the east and setting in the west. Let your clients get surprises another way. From you, more than anything, they want, need, and crave consistency.

Instead of delighting, celebrate. When you celebrate with your client, it is a bonding experience. It shows how far they've come, and how far you've come together. It reminds the client of their wins and how you saw them through a challenge. You'd be surprised that some of your clients' most important goals and successes go unnoticed by their loved ones, family, and friends. Often it's because these things aren't shared with those people in great detail. They don't understand all the hard work that went into launching a product, creating a new course, deciding how to go through a rebrand. Your client shares them with you, so share the celebration too.

You should always be thinking about the small steps you can take to provide a better experience for your clients. This includes gifting which we'll discuss in the next chapter.

Why "Done" is the Most Powerful Word in Your Vocabulary

No other word feels quite as good to say as "done." In Janet Choi's article "The Art of the Done List: Harnessing the Power of Progress," she explains why and how we should track the things we have done throughout the day. It serves as both a progress report and a motivational tool.

In a world of never-ending to-do lists, it's key to know what you've done and, more importantly, that what you have done matters. It's a great way to finish the day. You also should be using "done" as often as possible with your clients. As a virtual assistant, your job is not only to do the work but also to let the client know when it's completed. Don't diminish the win with long status checks and completion reports. No matter how you communicate with your client, no word in your vocabulary will have the same effect as "done."

Imagine yourself as your client. You've got meetings, you have ideas swirling around in your head, you have personal commitments, you have a ton of things you want and need to do. You have so much going on that it doesn't occur to you to stop and take a breath. At 100 miles an hour, you're in the zone. What could possibly stop you in your tracks, positively? To receive a message which simply says, "Done."

Merriam-Webster defines "done" as "arrived at or brought to an end." Reading or hearing that word stops people in their tracks. Why? Because being done means something is final. How many things in life and business are final?

The dictionary also defines "done" as physically exhausted. This is the reason hearing "done" lifts the weight. Business owners carry a weight with them even when something is delegated because as the leader, they are ultimately responsible for what does and doesn't get done. As soon as you let your client know that something is done, she can drop that weight. I have yet to meet someone who doesn't want to drop weight physically or metaphorically.

So where are we going wrong as virtual assistants? Our problems are oversharing, not being concise, sending too much information, and not allowing the business owner to celebrate what has been accomplished. What does this look like? It's the email that says what you completed and then lists what you are working on next. It's the text that says the work is finished and then asks several follow-up questions. It's the phone call where you tell your client what you did today and then quickly move on to next week's schedule.

While trying to use the time with your client wisely, you have just done the opposite. You haven't lifted the weight or the burden. On the contrary, you've added a fresh load without letting them take anything off.

What is the solution? Simply say, type, text, email "Done" and walk away. You'll be tempted to possibly add "congratulations" or "talk soon" or some other form of conversation. Don't! Let the power of done sink in and marinate. Plan to get your questions, next steps, or follow-up later. In the moment, all your client needs is the space to drop the weight and feel good that something is done. They no longer have to think about it, hold it in the back of their minds, or ask you for an update. Using "done" wisely will make you more valuable than you can imagine.

Summary

Managing Yourself

- Managing yourself is a crucial component of being a business owner. The most important rule of managing yourself is setting boundaries with yourself and the client.

- Loving what you do doesn't make you immune from burnout, and you can even become addicted to your work. Watch for signs before it happens and make sure you are taking time off regularly to disconnect.

- Even with regular disconnect days, you can still get into a "funk." Know how to reset yourself and what centers you again. Being in a funk usually means you have gotten away from yourself.

Managing the Client

- Educating your clients is an essential component of your business. Make sure you know how to do so effectively.

- There is a difference between people-pleasing and people-serving. We are in the people-serving business. You'll never be able to manage the client if you're only focused on pleasing them.

- You can't manage something without knowing what end result is desired. Know how the end result should be achieved and deliver the experience the client desires.

- Never underestimate the power of "done." Lift the client's burden and give them the room to breathe with a single word.

You can't manage clients if you can't manage yourself. The better you know yourself, the better you'll be able to serve your clients. These are crucial elements of your business and too often they get pushed under the rug because we get so focused on the day's work. Don't allow yourself to fall into that trap. Your business does not consist only of work and neither does your client's.

Once you are managing yourself and the client successfully, you now can begin to grow your business. Growing can be painful if you don't do it in the right order and in the right way. In fact, it's during growth where most VAs find they need to quit and start over again because they never learned to manage their business. Since you are going to grow the right way, we can concentrate on your growth drivers and how and when to spend money.

CHAPTER 7

Step 7: Growing Your Business

Don't wish for overnight success. Your business cannot support it anyway.

> *"Beautiful things are hard of attainment."*
>
> *—Plato*

Are You Priming Your Business for Success?

Running a business takes a lot of work. You work at it in order to achieve the level of success you desire, to meet the goals you've laid out, and to reach your dreams. However, the final piece is making sure you're in a place to receive. Have you thought about how you've primed your business for success?

When I think of primer, I think of painting. Applying a primer is one of the most important steps you can take before actually putting new color on the wall. Often it's the difference between having a flawless paint job and something that simply looks okay. It can be time consuming to prime the walls for paint, but the results cannot be ignored. Priming prepares the surface to receive the paint, the true color.

While in Barcelona, I was shopping for new lipstick. The makeup artist and I spoke at length about what kind I wear. I rattled off a list of all the reasons I can't wear the lipstick colors I did when I was younger. She patiently listened as I ran through the very long list. When I was finished, she didn't show me the latest or greatest products. Nor did she dismiss what I had told her. Instead, she asked a simple question, "You aren't using a primer, are you?" My puzzled response was, "No." To which she smiled and told me how a primer would fix all the issues I was having.

We walked over to the chair. She primed my lips and then put on this amazing red color that I never thought I would be able to wear again. She was right—the color was the same on me as it was in the tube. Flawless. And it remained the same throughout the entire day.

I remember walking out of the store, feeling amazing, even young again. I wondered how I could have gone so many years without knowing about primer for my lips. What else should I be priming? Why didn't I think of this before?

Well, the second question is much easier to answer. It's because I didn't think I needed it. Over the years, things have changed and I simply chalked it up to age. Instead of looking for a solution to my lipstick problems, I went the route of adapting and changing. That's what we're supposed to do, right? There was a problem with that answer though. The makeup artist was at least 15 years younger than I am, and she was using the same primer.

Again, a primer is used to prepare something to receive. Not simply receive but receive true, flawless results. I began thinking of my business. It makes sense to prime it. Priming isn't the same as laying the foundation. That's already been done. I'm priming my business to receive what I will get from achieving success. Priming will complement my core business principles (foundation) to receive the true results I desire.

I challenge you to think about the difference between getting and receiving. Getting things usually comes with a set of challenges and obstacles. It's called work for a reason. Receiving is not like work at all. When we receive, it is as if we are being gifted.

In this section, we're going to discuss the ways you can easily prime your business for not simply growth but being primed for success. Many of us are relentless and tenacious. We hit the goals we set for ourselves. However, we're not always as good at preparing to receive what we achieve from success. Since we know nothing is going to come between us and our business goals, preparing to receive seems like an unnecessary step. Failure is not an option.

Receiving the gifts of your business is important because if you keep giving and never receive, you'll get what you want and be miserable. I see it all the time. The VA with a thriving business, and they are walking away from it because they built, grew, and generated income for a company they built. They got everything they wanted and received nothing. No joy. No excitement. No plans to even have time for themselves. This isn't the business I want for you, and I know you don't want this either.

Start with being brutally honest with yourself. When you began your business, you might have struggled with the workload and the workflow. Unless you have mastered this now, you are not ready to grow. Instead you will implode and your clients will be the casualties along the way. This is bad for the client, your reputation, your business, your wallet, and the VA profession.

Growing your business should be about you. Your needs. Your family's needs. However, when someone is paying you to meet those needs, it's no longer just about you. It's also about your client, their family, their reputation, their business, and their wallet too. I can't stress enough that every decision you make should be a win-win for you and your clients. If your business growth only helps you, your client is losing.

The first step to growing is actually scaling back, planning for the unexpected growing pains. We all have them, and while you can't know what they will be, you can buffer some time for it. You do this by planning your workload and scheduling for your worst day, not your best.

I suffer from migraines. I take medicine, but it doesn't always work. If I had deadlines to meet every single day, I would be in big trouble. If I didn't schedule time for breaks, I wouldn't be able to work at a slower pace. If I worked on an hourly fee basis, I couldn't afford to take a day off and make it up later. Certainly traveling the world would be out of the question.

If you have every minute of your workday planned out without breaks and buffered time, you will run into problems. If you are scheduling yourself to work 40 hours a week now, how can you grow? Is your goal to work 60 or 80 hours? If so, you're well on your way. I recommend setting a 30-hour-a-week schedule for your client load. If you're not a general or executive VA and you're more project-based, I recommend scheduling Fridays off, either for pleasure or as a growth day.

I must be fully transparent and let you know I work a lot. I love my work. (Remember I'm trying not to be addicted to it.) However, my work is growing my business. The time I spend on client work is far less than I spend on growing my business, launching products, being coached, and writing. If I worked more than 30 hours a week on clients, I wouldn't have time for myself. Often client work is only 20 hours a week.

Also, no one is better at scheduling time off than me. When I look at my calendar and see what I'm doing and what's in the pipeline, I'm honest with myself about how much I'll be working. I take into consideration the stress factors as well. Not all work is equal. In doing so, I know how to plan my time off accordingly.

At the beginning of 2017, I was going strong. I worked a lot to launch my virtual summit and then to be ready to launch my online pilot course. Still, in March, only a few weeks out from the summit, I took three days off and completely disconnected. When it seemed like I didn't have the time to rest is when I needed it the most. I was glad I did.

In late May, after the summit ended, business was booming and I had factored in all the follow-ups and work to be done. Then I went on a planned vacation for a full 11 days. This gave me enough time to field all the emails and calls from the summit, manage my clients, get the online class started, and then let everyone know I would be on vacation. It was seamless.

In July, I completed the online class and vacationed with my family in Berlin. In August, my work was completed. I had VAs working for me to begin new projects, and I started working with a marketing and branding strategist. I worked less than 20 hours a week during August on both my business and client work.

In September, I took a week off to travel to Israel and then a few days at the end of the month I took time off to visit Dubai. In November, I took several days off to visit Hong Kong. During these times away from work, I was earning exactly what I do while I'm working a non-vacation schedule. These last three trips were in the middle of writing and editing this book. I couldn't pass up the opportunities to travel.

Each time I take on a new client or project, I have to consider my time and my value. I also immediately determine when my next time off will be. For 2017, launching two products for the first time and writing my second book—all in one year—I knew there was going to be a lot of long, stressful days. Instead of doing this from my home in the middle of the country, I chose to do it while traveling to 16 countries. I run the same business regardless of where I am. However, traveling reminds me to do things my way, allows me to stay far away from burnout, and is exciting to talk about with clients.

All Answers Come from Questions

Business relationships are not that different from personal relationships. You and your closest friends probably speak a language all your own. You might be able to finish one another's sentences and have inside jokes no one else understands. To get to this place in a business relationship can seem challenging, especially when you grow or are leveling up. This is new territory.

As Jeffrey Shaw (who I previously mentioned in chapter 5) said, he had to trust his instincts because "you don't know what you don't know." He didn't know the simple act of not using tape when wrapping gifts for his ideal clients was going to be the catalyst that changed everything in his business, but he trusted his instincts. The only thing he knew was Bergdorf Goodman didn't use it and his family used a lot of it.

He knew he was entering into a luxury market and he didn't know anything about being rich. In desperation, he was forced to seek out answers to questions he didn't have. Even if you are not desperate, taking on new clients, or have a full client load, it's your duty to grow mentally and to expand on your current way of thinking. If you don't, you run the risk of becoming complacent. Additionally, your work can become outdated and clients will not be served. While you search for answers without knowing the questions, there are questions you should be asking yourself each month to prompt curiosity.

Ask yourself these seven questions every month:

What did I commit to?

If you're not committing to anything, then why are you in business? You need to make commitments to yourself and your business. This could be to expand your referral network, make two more client calls a day, secure one more client a month, etc. Successful VAs don't wait for business to come—

they create, develop, and expand. Don't want to expand? Take a class, learn a skill. Think about the idea of being able to raise your rates and do less while providing more.

What did I actually do?

We can't let ourselves become our best clients. If you don't have enough time in the day, why? Are you overcommitted? Not motivated enough? Burned out? Examine the work you're doing, the clients you have, and your prices to see where you can improve. Don't forget your answer might be hiring a VA. If you don't believe in the investment of a virtual assistant, then why should someone hire you?

What worked?

VAs need to constantly test what is working and what isn't. Did you find calling clients gave you a better response rate than emailing? Were your infographics more engaging than your written content? Are you testing content on your website, blog, and social media channels to find out where your clients are coming from? Don't guess. Test and analyze.

What didn't work?

If something didn't work, do another test or try A/B testing to determine if it's not the right content or platform. Only when you have found what works can you stop testing. Lack of engagement or failure doesn't prove your theory. Only success can do that. Remember to fail fast and forget about your undead ideas.

What's next?

Remember, as a business owner you are in sales. Each month you need to be looking down the road at the next several months to determine how you are going to gain new clients and/or manage the clients you have. It is your job to project and then plan accordingly. Your bottom line depends on it. Growth requires a plan.

What was your biggest challenge this month?

This doesn't have to be business related. We have personal lives and families. Whatever challenge you have, you need to address it. Trying to dismiss it won't make it go away. Do you need to cut back your workload? Do you need to raise your prices and reduce your client work? Make the hard decisions now while you're in control of the situation. If not, the situation will take control of you.

What was your biggest win of the month?

If you don't take the time to celebrate your wins, you are hurting yourself. Being a business owner is not always easy, and your clients may not validate your work in the way you want them to. Celebrate yourself! Even if it was getting out of your comfort zone to make a sales call, sending a proposal for work you've never done before, reaching out to your potential dream client, or breaking even for the first time. These are things to celebrate. You are winning! Every month you can look back at your achievements, you'll be able to track how far you've come. It's a wonderful feeling!

How do you become an elite VA? Well, you don't copy others. You have high standards and keep growing them. No elite business ever kept banking hours. Think about that. Now this doesn't mean you are on call 24/7 unless that is your business and you are being appropriately compensated. How much can you really charge when you are doing what everyone else is doing and not providing anything extra?

Why can some retailers charge more than others? Service. To go above and beyond for a customer is included in a business's service and price. When I worked at Nordstrom, I was allowed to do whatever I wanted to make the customer happy. To some companies, that is scary. To Nordstrom, it is their policy. This included hand-delivering packages to the customer's home. Bringing a pressed tuxedo shirt to someone's car after taking the credit card information over the phone. And, yes, it also meant accepting returns.

Working at Nordstrom was a lot like waiting on tables when I was young. The better service I gave, the more money I made. As a waitress I made $2.10 an hour (the legal minimum wage for servers) and the rest came from tips. You'd better believe I was doing everything I could to get a good tip. As a salesperson at Nordstrom, I worked on a commission-only basis. I was frequently the best salesperson in my department and among the top ten salespersons in the store. However, I couldn't sell just anything—only what the customers needed and wanted. Remember, they can return *anything*, and then my commission would have been taken away.

If you can't provide five-star service and work outside of regular business hours to serve your client from time to time, you are not ready to grow. The CEO of a company with 10,000 employees and the CEO of a company with 30,000 employees can't operate the same. Throw in an international presence, and now you've just upped the stakes. I can also assure you these CEOs are not compensated the same either.

To be clear, when I talk about growing your business, I mean an elite business. I don't mean growing it like a McDonald's chain. The world doesn't need another McDonald's. I'm talking about growing a business the same way you would a fancy boutique retail store—one that is located in only certain cities. Sure, you could open another McDonald's anywhere, and people will come in to grab a bite. Or you could open the equivalent of a boutique store and have customers seek you out and plan their shopping trips around your business.

Client Referrals and Gifting

Some of the most iconic and high-priced brands don't participate in traditional advertising and marketing. They don't need to. Their businesses are based on their current client base and referrals. People aspire to be able to afford these brands because it means they have reached a certain status. For others, like myself, it means I get to have the experience of shopping with that company. I want that level of service, and I literally can't wait to write a blog post or share it with the world.

If you have grown your business and aren't receiving client referrals, there is a reason. It could be as simple as not asking, but there is always a reason.

Client referrals and gifting go hand in hand. You don't do one to get the other. This isn't scratch my back and I'll scratch yours. It is how you keep and retain long-term relationships. It's what separates you from the competition.

You want to do gifting because it's how your clients know they are appreciated, long after money has changed bank accounts. Referrals are what clients send your way for not only what you do but *how* you do it. We love and dream of the coveted referral and yet can repel it at the same time.

When someone receives a referral from a friend or colleague, she is expecting to be treated as a VIP. That's the point of being referred—so you don't get treated like everyone else. Who doesn't want to jump to the front of the line, bypass paperwork and forms, or be offered a service while you wait? Think about how often you give referrals. Why do you give them? How excited are you to share a great service when someone asks?

If you're like me, you don't give them all the time because not every service deserves them. I only give referrals when I have received *exceptional* service. The opportunity to share a referral happens quickly through a tweet or a reply on Facebook or LinkedIn. However I share a referral, the point is I feel like I'm about to make someone else's life easier or better. If someone came back to me with an awful experience about my referral, I would be extremely embarrassed and most likely never refer the business or service or again.

Referring isn't just about putting the business's reputation on the line. You are putting yours on the line as well. If the level of service doesn't meet someone's expectations, they may not tell the business, but they are very likely to share it with the person who referred them. No one wants to be on the receiving end of that conversation.

Searching out and hiring a virtual assistant is no different. It is a very personal matter, even though it's business related. A business owner is about to let someone they will never meet into their daily life, their means of supporting themselves and their family, something they've been building and growing. Receiving a referral relieves some of the anxiety of finding a VA on their own.

We are in the virtual assistance business. Often we forget what it is like to be an outsider to our very familiar world. Having someone referred to you doesn't make their fears, worries, or doubts go away. It only lessens them. Client referrals are a way for you to show someone how having a VA can still be personal and tailored to them.

Notice I used the word "can." It's because you are given the opportunity. Too often I see VAs miss the mark on referrals. The way we all want to get our business is exactly the way you are losing out on business.

Be sure you're not doing these four thing that can ruin your referral business:

You can ruin the experience when you think the referral is a slam dunk.

What happened to the personal service? Where did the excitement go? Whoever referred a potential client to you most likely listed these traits as what attracted and keeps her using your services in the first place. So treat your potential clients as you would every other person who reaches out to you (assuming you do this well). Give her your undivided attention. Treat her as if she's the only one who matters right now. Don't cut corners and assume the person who referred her has done all the work for you. What that person has done is conveyed an experience—an experience the potential client also wants to have. Provide the same tailored experience, and she'll say "yes" to becoming one of your clients.

You ruin the experience by taking a long time to respond.

When you wait too long to reach out to a potential client, you have just made the person feel like another number. They can get this type of service anywhere. The reason they are even looking for referrals is to skip this feeling altogether. You are also assuming this person hasn't contacted anyone else.

Respond right away to any request from a potential client, if not immediately. Even if it is to say you aren't free until next week. If someone is looking for virtual assistance, you can bet they have a busy schedule too. Get on their calendar before someone else does. A slow response brings no hope for the future. Show how thoughtful you are and how much their time means to you. In doing so, they can feel valued and appreciated from the beginning.

You ruin the experience by not showing gratitude.

Someone went out of her way to not only compliment your work but to send a potential client your way. If the same person sent you a check in the mail, would you not so much as send a thank you card? Even if you don't end up working with the person they referred, you should express some form of appreciation. It is basic common courtesy.

Send a thank you card or pick up the phone to express true gratitude. If the potential client is a great fit for you, encourage the referrer to continue sending similar clients your way. Should it be a wrong fit, let the person know how much you appreciate the thought and who would make a good referral going forward.

After you sign the potential client, send a gift to the referrer. It could be a percentage of the contract you signed or lunch, dinner, or drinks on your dime. The list is endless. The point is, successful referrals should never go unnoticed. Most importantly, don't forget to ask how you can help the referrer in return. Don't assume you know their needs. They might be starting a new venture or looking for a service or product completely unrelated to what you offer. Do you have a contact in your network they want to be introduced to? This is an opportunity for you to build on your relationship and grow trust. Give back!

You ruin the experience by not marketing your services and being visible.

Just because someone referred you doesn't mean the potential client isn't going to look you up. When they do, what will they find? Are you a blogger who hasn't updated your own blog in months? Is your website outdated? No one wants to find out a potential virtual assistant doesn't have enough time to maintain her own information. It inspires no confidence.

Keep your website, social media presence, and blog current. You never know who might come across your work, but you can determine what they find. Be proud of what you are sharing and posting online.

Client referrals could be the best thing for your business. As with all things in your business, you should have a plan—a plan for handling referrals, conducting follow-up, and attracting more referrals. Gifting and referrals go hand in hand.

Gifting should never be confused with SWAG (stuff we all get). Never give promotional gifts with your logo on them. And most importantly, don't give gifts expecting to get something in return. John Ruhlin is the gifting expert. Read his book *Giftology* to find a complete list of items never to give, even if you follow these rules. You can also check out the link in the Resources section of your workbook.

No matter how much you're making, you should have a budget for gifting clients. Think about every element of the gift experience—the way the client will receive the gift, how it will look when the client opens the gift. Is the card handwritten? Did you ask for a referral or include a business card? Don't! This means it's no longer a gift.

I challenge you to take your gifting offline. Be different. Receiving an e-card and a physical card aren't the same. Know your audience. If they do their best to be a completely paperless company, a physical card might not be the best fit. Also, be different by staying away from business products. If you have absolutely no budget, there is still a way to gift. You could offer a service free of charge. You could donate your time to their favorite charity. Create a special thank you video for them. There is a way to show your appreciation.

Don't Duplicate Yourself. You Need to Complete the Puzzle.

In conversation, something that often comes up is the desire to duplicate ourselves. "If only there were two of me. I could work twice as much, make twice as much money, come up with twice as many ideas, work twice as many hours." This is not at all appealing to me. The last thing I need is another me, and the last thing you need is another you.

Here's why. Another you only creates more work. Another you would only have more great ideas, see more opportunity, and willingly seek out new clients. And in the end, you'll still need help getting it all done. Ideas need to be refined, tested, and systematized to work. Opportunity takes time and money and uses a lot of your critical thinking to determine the real costs. Sure, clients bring in more money, but they take up more time as well. You have to devote quality time to their needs as well as follow-up, surveys, programming, and so on.

No one ever says, "I wish I could duplicate myself so the first me could make the money and strategize so the other me can do the paperwork, manage the details, and create a system." More importantly, no one ever says the duplicate version of themselves would take a vacation and spend more time with family, take a day off, relax. And dare I say have a lazy day?

The idea to duplicate one's self is often premature. First, you need to complete the puzzle. Where are you coming up short? Where is your time being wasted? What do you simply not want to do? What keeps you from your genius zone, your writing, your clients? What is keeping you up at night? What piece of the puzzle do you need to find to pull everything together before you duplicate?

Think of duplication as franchising. You franchise a business after you have put an exact system and process in place. The customers are purchasing the company's method of success. A guarantee. Are you franchisable? What guarantee could you give someone if you offered them a duplicate version of yourself? As Michael E. Gerber—bestselling author of *The E-Myth* and what *The Wall Street Journal* calls the No. 1 business book of all time—says, "A business's mission is always to create the system."

This is a very common reason clients hire me—to find a virtual assistant who can help them create a system. A funnel system. An email drip system. To write out a process for what it is they do exactly. Business owners go from helping one client to helping many. Then they realize they don't have a failproof system. Something is always falling through the cracks. Nor is there a timeline to complete the tasks. If it's a good week, they can take care of things right away. If it's a busy week or if they are traveling, emails get pushed off and lost. They scramble to find what they need to send, let alone have time to create something new. Don't think because you are a VA and specialize in these things that you are immune from them.

Think of yourself as the CEO of your company because you are. Now imagine you have a team working for you. Who would be the first people to hire as your top executives? Who would be your first hire not on your leadership team? In what areas could you use another person's assistance? Everything you tell your clients applies to you. You can't do it all yourself. You shouldn't be doing it all yourself.

When Is It Time to Hire Support? Watch for the Signs

Knowing when to hire support seems easy enough. Most people would recommend hiring help when you no longer can do everything yourself. Of course, the help would be valuable at the time. However, you're late in hiring and you've already cost yourself a lot of undue stress.

Think about it. You would never tell someone to start exercising *after* their physician prescribes medication. Changing your diet isn't best *after* you've already taken a scary trip to the emergency room. The best time for help is *before* you need it. Preventative maintenance.

As VAs we can be the worst offenders. We want to do everything ourselves, learn all the ins and outs, be the expert of everything. Sometimes it is to your benefit to do this, but most of the time it isn't. You need to think like a CEO. If you were building a brick and mortar business and could save money by doing some of the manual labor yourself, are you really saving money? Did you take into consideration the cost to rent the location, the expenses being held, the delay in being able to promote the location, being sidetracked with different work, and ultimately not bringing in a dollar? Hiring is investing. Sound familiar? Is this an investment in your business or a "nice to have?" If it's a "nice to have," then yes, you should consider whether or not to pay someone else.

I couldn't wait to hire VAs to help support my business. I, like my clients, want to throw money at problems because we want to see them fixed now. Any problem I have is a direct roadblock to a client reaching me, to an experience I can give to a client, to money in my bank account.

I knew from the beginning who my first hire was going to be. A bookkeeper. After that I had some ideas, but I was open. At any given time, I have two to five VAs working for me. When people ask how I get so much done and how I can achieve so many goals in a single year while traveling the world, I tell them that I take my own advice and hire VAs. Remember in the beginning I told you to create mile markers? This was one of mine. When I reached a specific point in my business, I was going to hire a bookkeeper. And I did!

Once on a call with a client, we discovered that his time was worth about $800 an hour. He was giving an hour a week to a client who was only bringing in $5,000 a year. He was losing over $40,000 a year, one hour at a time. Now we don't all make $800 an hour (yet!). But what is costing you an hour at a time over the course of a year? Who could you do what you're doing for less money?

One of the biggest hesitations business owners have is not knowing if they have enough steady work to hire someone. They think in terms of 20 or 40 hours a week. Rarely does anyone need a virtual assistant for this many hours. That's a lot! The norm is five to ten hours a week, ten being on the high side. Remember you're a business owner now too. The same rules apply.

Watch for these signs that may indicate you're ready to hire help:

- **You are unable to manage your calendar successfully.** It's a problem if you don't have time to schedule appointments with clients or potential clients. It's an even bigger problem when you don't have personal time to schedule or attend your routine doctor appointments. Ignoring how you spend time on your calendar is like ignoring the amount of money you have in the bank. Don't become overdrawn!

- **Every new client has you scrambling**. You scramble to send the proposal, send the invoice, schedule the meetings, and then fit in the work.

- **Everything you want to implement seems months and years away**. One of my favorite questions to ask during client consultations is "What have you wanted to implement in your business but haven't yet?"

If you aren't ready to hire help for your business, you might benefit from help for your personal life. Think about hiring a food delivery service, a housekeeping service, a lawn service, a laundry service, or some other help for your home life. What could you do to make your life easier so you can enjoy your time off from work more? Take a look at your client load, your services, and your prices immediately. You might need to redo your business model so you can keep up the pace and feel fulfilled in both your work life and your home life.

Be honest with yourself. If you were your client, what would you tell yourself? The signs are all there. If you choose to ignore them, you'll face the consequences later. When you decide to stop, listen, and take action, all the signs start pointing in a positive direction for your business. CEO-level thinking will get you to CEO-level lifestyle and money.

Reevaluating Success

Another critical step to growing your business is reevaluating success. And you do need to reevaluate. When your business reaches a level of success, then you need to redefine success. You achieved it, now you need to set your sights on something else, even if it's simply maintaining your success. Again, your level of success doesn't have to be something grand by anyone's standards. It has to be something valuable and important to *you*.

All growth brings change. Even slight shifts create huge changes. Before you begin to grow and take the physical steps to the next level, take out your business plan. Look it over thoughtfully. What did you start out saying you wanted? What did you achieve? What changed? What do you want now?

We often talk about businesses—our clients' and ours—like being our babies. When your children say their first word, take their first steps, start to be able to feed themselves, these are all monumental moments. However, as they grow, you don't keep taking photos and videos and celebrating those same monumental moments. The natural growth and progression now has you awaiting the next first—the first day of school, the first dance, the first time driving, the first date. You don't want to take first events for granted. They are basic but necessary motor skills. However, you have automatically reevaluated what your children's next successes will be.

Your business is talking, walking, and feeding itself. Now you need to reevaluate who you wish to talk with, walk alongside, and provide value to. Will it still be serving just a few clients, or are you ready to move to serving many clients? Are you happy where you are? If so, that's fine, but don't make the mistake of being stagnant. The smallest body of water will stay fresh with a small stream of flowing water. The largest body of water will become polluted with none.

One area you may overlook for reevaluation is your ideal client. However, it is the most necessary. If you mirror your clients and you've changed, doesn't it make sense that your clients have changed too? This is a perfect opportunity to go through your client and consultation list and see who you've been attracting, who you're working with, and most importantly who you've turned away.

What if you need to change your ideal client? Before you decide to change, consider adding another client. Coca-Cola didn't only create a positive phenomenon with its "Share a Coke" campaign. In 1985 the iconic company that had been in business for 99 years announced it would discontinue the original flavored Coke and would introduce "New Coke." It was a disaster so big it's still taught in business schools today as what not to do. The company feared cannibalization if they offered both Original and New Coke.

With backlash worldwide—yep, even Fidel Castro weighed in on the conversation—ABC World News Tonight anchor Peter Jennings interrupted a soap opera to break the story—Original Coke was coming back. Here's the clincher, though—Coca-Cola didn't get rid of New Coke. They renamed Original Coke to Coca-Cola Classic. New Coke remained in production until 2002.

How does this relate to your business? Be careful before you decide to get rid of what built your business. If Coke failed to do this successfully, we all need to be careful. Instead, label your original service as your "classic" option. Of course, that is metaphorical. Your verbiage should be in your ideal client's language. Even if you no longer sell that original service, potential clients may be finding you through that service. So don't get rid of it! Consider it your lead magnet. A good lead magnet is hard to come by!

In the beginning of growth, only add; don't take away. Once you start turning away customers and clients, it is very hard to get them back if your new plan does not work out. If it does, a smart business owner and CEO finds a way to convert those potential clients into sales. But if you know those clients do not represent the direction you're going, then be smart. Offer to consult on or manage the project. If all else fails, find someone else to serve them. You might even get a referral fee.

Since executive and virtual assistants are the worker bees in the working world, in the beginning we think that we'll continue in this role as our businesses grow. But you can't. You grew in the beginning. And now it's time for scaling. You have become the person who is in demand. Now it's a privilege to work with you. You're not taking on new clients, but you've moved to private consulting. Do you see where I'm going with this?

What if you don't want to consult? Do you want to train? If so, who wants to pay to learn from you? Remember, you're changing your ideal client. Your mirror shows something different when you look into it now. If you are a teacher, now the mirror should show you your ideal students. If you are a consultant, the mirror should show you a different type of client. Now follow the money trail to create your ideal client all over again.

It can be trickier the second time around. The people who need your help might not be able to afford you. Believe me, this is a hard pill to swallow when all you want to do is help people. Remember that free, valuable lead magnet? That's for those people. Is it valuable enough to help those who can't afford you? If not, step up your value game. Never forget that when you're growing a business, you should have more to donate—more time and more money. Don't give what you don't have. Donate what you have an excess of.

One of the pitfalls of business is trying to get things perfect before we launch. But perfect doesn't exist. In fact, it is your clients who can perfect it for you. Create pilot courses or programs, then ask former clients to test the pilots for you. People love being the first to try new things and products. Be very specific in your ask—explain why you chose them to test this product, what you want in return, and how you want to receive it. Otherwise you will get nothing in return. These people like you. They don't know how forward or candid they should be, nor do they know what your desired outcome is until you explain it.

One of the struggles of growing your business is trying to do so in a linear way. Nothing is ever that simple. To grow you have to have a following. Your following will tell you exactly what they need. Perfect! Offer it. Other times your following doesn't know and you have to think it through for them. They have a lot going on. Listen to what they're saying, what they're doing, and most importantly where they're spending their time and money. It's all theory until someone pays for something.

So how do you build your following? First, you need to give them a path to follow. Start dropping breadcrumbs. When a lot of people start to pick up the crumbs, create a roadmap and put up the signs.

I was unknowingly doing this in my own business, and I bet you are too. I love to write, so I spent a lot of my time writing, and my clients were finding me through my writing. My clients were aspiring authors, and they pressed me to write my own book. They were looking at me to mirror them. One day I decided I would, and I did. The book was for the client and the potential client. I never could have guessed it would present an opportunity to expand my business the way it did.

What I was hoping to do was gain more matchmaking clients. This book did that and so much more! It also opened the doors for me to consult, create a summit, write an online course, and eventually write this book. Sure, it makes sense now, but it didn't at the time. Another bonus was signing a huge contract with a single client who already knew my time commitment. I attracted him, and he is my ideal.

I call them breadcrumbs because they shouldn't cost you a lot of time and energy. You shouldn't be putting all your eggs in one basket. You simply never know what people want and will pay for until they do. What are the breadcrumbs and road signs that are directing people to you? Make sure it is free, helpful, valuable information.

Why would I tell you not to monetize your giveaway? Because what you're offering is the real business model to build on. You'll only be able to charge so much for a giveaway, and it won't position your business ahead of anyone else's. It won't create another income stream but a mere drip. Those who have nothing more to offer than what they're selling have nothing to give for free. When you have a free giveaway, you're telling the potential client that the best is yet to come.

How does giving away free, helpful, valuable information help you build a following? That free giveaway will help you create an email list. Don't give anything away to anyone without collecting a piece of their information first. Building email lists is all the rage, and you can buy countless classes and summits to help you build your list. I endorse none of them. However, I believe you do need to build your list of potential customers, clients, and most importantly evangelists—people who will promote you and your business whether or not they can afford your services.

Now think about the breadcrumbs you've already been throwing out. Breadcrumbs are your content. Are you a podcaster, a writer, a speaker, a webinar host? The right one is a combination of something your clients want and something you love to do. Whatever you do, do it daily in the beginning. Think of it like compound interest. You don't have to push it out daily, but you should get in the habit of devoting daily time to it. That is how you grow in leaps and bounds later. The point is to create some kind of momentum.

At this point in your career, I also suggest creating or joining a mastermind group. I don't recommend starting with a mastermind group because you first need a master plan. Joining too soon can actually be discouraging and not allow you to think through and process your ideas and your business goals. I've been in one long-term mastermind group, and I can tell you it's been a game changer. Had I joined before I was ready, I would have been crushed at what the others in the group were accomplishing while I was still working out the kinks of starting up my business.

Knowing what kind of mastermind group to join is key. You don't have to join a group where all of the members share the same field or industry. (You can be the only VA in the group.) Your ideal mastermind group should contain people who are committed to the group, have shared values and goals, and are open to constructive criticism. If you can't get real in your mastermind group, you can't get real anywhere. Also, I firmly believe you should be a little afraid of going back to the group if you haven't been doing the work in your business that you should be doing. It's not a successful mastermind group if the members make excuses for one another.

Besides finding these criteria in my mastermind group, I also leveled up. I joined a group that included women who were far more successful than me. They served as mentors and people I aspired to be like. Had I joined a group of women who were in the same place where I was in business, I wouldn't have been as driven to grow my business. To be clear, this was perception. I perceived that the members of my mastermind group were successful business owners based on how they presented themselves within the group. No one shared financial information. However, I could see that this group was full of people who were listed in *Forbes*, who speak at international conferences, who had social proof. That's what I was after.

When you get out of the habit of doing things in a linear way, you'll naturally have more opportunities to improve your business. Be careful when people want to partner with you. I'm a huge fan of partnering and collaborating. But I have a rule: *Would I trust this person with my children?* If I can't answer with a "yes," the answer is made for me. "No." Don't ever make the decision based on how you judge that person's character. No one is that good. This is business. Get everything in writing. That means you should have worked together on a previous project, know the other person's financials, contacted the person's references, and collected legal documentation to prove the validity of that person's business.

What's the fastest way to grow and make money? Hiring a business coach. I can't stress enough the importance of having the right coach. I make more money when I work with a coach. Period. That's their job. They take my natural skills and abilities and make me better. The best quarterback in the National Football League (NFL) has a coach. In fact, he has many coaches—head coach, quarterback coach, strength and conditioning coach, nutrition coach. You only need one coach to improve your game.

The First Time I Invested in a Business Coach, I Was Terrified

I remember the first meeting I had with my business coach. I never had one before, so I didn't know what to expect. We were meeting at Starbucks, which I thought was "safe." If the meeting didn't go well or if I became uncomfortable, I knew I could leave as soon as I finished my coffee. Except that didn't happen.

Our 30-minute coffee meeting turned into a two-hour discussion. I still remember her face when she looked down at her phone, discovered how much time had passed, and realized she was late to pick up her kids! Of course, there was no time for proper goodbyes as she rushed out the door.

Sitting there afterward, I was amazed. Who was this woman who knew all these things about me? It was like I just had coffee with a psychic. No one had ever understood me like that before. No one really understood what I wanted out of life or my business. How could they? I barely knew myself. What I wanted at the time, I wasn't even sure it existed and if it did, I surely didn't know how to obtain it. We joke now, but I tell people she had her work cut out for her when she started working with me. I wasn't at ground zero; I was subzero.

Later the next week, we had a formal call to talk about her services and what she could offer me. I wanted what she had. It was a six-month commitment, and it would cost me $5,000! What?! I was struggling to get clients. How was I going to pay that? How could I justify spending money that I wasn't even making? Something in my gut told me I wasn't going to get where I wanted to go on my own. Before the call, ended I made the commitment. Later that day, I submitted my credit card number and then wondered what in the world I had just done!

What I did was make a huge shift in my thinking. I had started thinking like a business owner. I made an investment in my product and what I was selling—me. It was the best thing I could have done. During the next six months, I began to work less and make more money doing what I loved. I signed a six-month $7,500 contract, which was my largest to date. Then I signed a few more $4,500 contracts. I was about to send out a $15,000 contract and my hand was shaking. I was terrified it would be rejected and I would lose the client. The proposal was already three times more than I had charged previously. I texted my coach, and we got on the phone. After talking with her, I raised the price to $21,000, and guess what? It was accepted! Throw in some other contracts, and I suddenly made over $40,000 in six months!

The biggest takeaway was I was working less and really enjoying what I was doing. No more cringing or rolling my eyes when I received a phone call or an email from a client who wasn't my ideal client. It didn't really feel like working. Since then I've never been without a coach or in a class of some sort. I always make more money when I invest in myself. Period.

I've included this in the growth section because not everyone will need a coach in the beginning. I did. It was the right time for me. You need to hire a coach at the right time for you and your business. I've met my fair share of VAs who were doing great right out of the gate and didn't hire a coach until they had a full client load and needed to diversify their income or raise their rates. Whether or not you hire a coach in the beginning, hire one during your growth phase. It is a must!

As you grow your business, it might become apparent that you are no longer a VA or an admin. That's okay. Don't fight it. This is your new career journey. The clients who need your services may not be looking for an assistant, but they are looking for what you offer. You'll be ahead of your competition because you'll already know how to operate and create your own systems and procedures.

Opportunity is a funny thing. I often hear VAs tell me the moment they finished a course on a specific topic or took a class on a certain software, they met someone who needed it. It's not simply by chance. When you prepare yourself for opportunities, you begin to see them everywhere. What are you prepared for? What have you been wanting to do and haven't done yet? Instead of planning for every crisis, plan for every opportunity.

Marketing

When is the right time to invest in marketing? It took me almost three years to invest in marketing, and it all started with a marketing and branding strategist coach. The first year I was in business was pretty much a comedy of errors, except I wasn't laughing. Marketing right out of the gate is never a smart idea. Chances are you don't have a clear statement, vision, customer identity, and value proposition. I think I changed business cards three times in the first two years! Business cards are cheap. Marketing is expensive!

Another reason to hold off on marketing in the beginning is because one of the struggles businesses face in marketing are what Jeffrey Shaw calls "breaks in communication." How we communicate across a multitude of platforms commonly has disconnects. We sound one way on paper, another on video, and yet another in ads. Rarely do we "show up" the way we think we're supposed to.

Companies will have you believe it is as simple as putting your name in a publication. Social media and digital marketers want you to believe crafting the right ad will work to bring people to your business. You could spend thousands of dollars on marketing, and you might even get some results. I recommend you don't promote marketing for your business in the beginning because what you have is not what you'll end up with. Therefore, the money you spend on marketing is most likely going to be wasted.

If you're going to invest in anything, invest in yourself. Invest in your content. When is it time to invest? When you're confident you have the right path, have a following, and have exhausted all of your free resources. After I worked with a coach, I spent money on consulting services with a marketing strategist. I didn't do this until I was confident I had done everything in my power, exhausted every free resource, read the books, tried and tested my audience, and was going to hit a wall or, worse, go stagnant.

When I joined Self-Publishing School, that was the most expensive thing I had purchased for my business, besides coaching. I was joining because they answered all my questions. I knew what I was getting and how what they offered fit into my vision for my business.

When purchasing anything for your business, ask yourself when the investment will pay off. How many clients would you need to bring on board to break even on your costs? Know why you're paying money for a service or commodity. Are you paying for someone's expertise and knowledge, for accountability, for their service, for connections and a community? Any one of these responses is acceptable. However, if you don't know why you're purchasing something, you will forget why it's valuable, regret spending the money, and ultimately not follow through on using the item you purchased.

Getting Out of Your Comfort Zone Doesn't Have to Be Painful

"Life begins at the end of your comfort zone."

—Neale Donald Walsch

As a notebook lover, I've seen this quote on the cover of several notebooks and journals. It makes sense. You could very well be writing down some things that cause discomfort. Being the kind of person who buys a new notebook or journal for each new project or adventure, I know this quote by heart. Honestly, it's one of my many favorites. For the longest time, I didn't truly understand what it meant.

For some reason, I associated doing new things and trying new growth opportunities as being not just uncomfortable but painful. Like a child ripping off a Band-Aid, everything I did was to hope the pain could be taken all at once and not be a long, drawn out process. I'm not sure where I ever got the idea that being uncomfortable also had to be painful. It is natural to be uncomfortable. It is not natural for it to painful.

I realized that quote doesn't say anything about pain. It mentions "comfort." When I started marketing, I went into it like a dreaded trip to the dentist's office. Being no stranger to hours in the dentist chair, I remembered all the things my dentist told me in the past. "This is going to sting a little." "You should feel pressure, but raise your hand if you feel pain." "Is it sensitive or painful to cold or heat?" The sting, pressure, or sensitivity to things outside our comfort zones in normal. Pain is not.

When I wrote my first book, I certainly stretched outside my comfort zone. Writing this book didn't bring the same discomfort as the first. Although this book is for a different audience, I am not challenged by the same things I was while writing my first book. For that project, I was most concerned with hitting the "publish" button. I couldn't imagine anything scarier. Unfortunately, I didn't allow myself to think of anything positive either. If I had, the experience would have been completely different.

This time around my goal was to write better than before. My message is solid. What keeps me up at night is getting the message out—a.k.a. the marketing. I had visions of my face plastered on frisbees and bus benches, littering Facebook with ads, and spamming people like a Nigerian princess. You know, basically, everything that makes you want to put someone's face up on a dart board and hit the bullseye. That's painful, right?

I thought all those things even though I knew I would never market myself like that. I couldn't shake the traditional methods, new methods, latest trends, and what everyone was telling me to do. And by everyone I mean every email and ad that comes in the form of pop-ups and spam. Then it hit me like a ton of bricks. (Because it's metaphorical, it wasn't actually painful!) *Do what you love!* You may have to do it in a new way, but do what you love.

Sharing my knowledge and educating people is the best part of my day. The joy I receive is unprecedented, and it never gets old. Could I do this in marketing—provide exceptional value and stay true to myself? You bet I can! What will keep me going even though I'm uncomfortable? Knowing you will benefit.

Stretch yourself outside of your comfort zone. Expect to be uncomfortable. In the beginning you might not even be that great at it. That's okay! Think back to the pilot of your favorite television show. Then think of the finale. Your favorite actors got better because they stretched themselves. Don't shy away from discomfort, but avoid pain.

Are You Taking Advice from the Right Person?

The world of virtual assistants is growing. There is no shortage of experts and coaches to tell you what to do. However, being a virtual assistant isn't their career. Most have no administrative background of any kind. So why are you taking advice from them?

Simply hiring a VA or using a service does not make someone an expert. Why? Because it's a one-sided deal. The person is only looking out for their needs, not the virtual assistant's needs. Additionally, they have no idea what goes into the work and what to look for. There is more to being a virtual assistant than checking tasks off a to-do list.

If they are successful entrepreneurs, why throw their hats in the VA game? For many, the short answer is to make a buck or maybe millions of them. It's what makes them entrepreneurs. There's a lot of money to be made in the field of virtual assistance as it continues to grow. But I am doubtful these experts have a passion for the profession.

So whose advice are you following? What do you want from them? Are they coaches? Are they consultants? And yes, there's a difference. What is their specialization or niche? Are you their ideal client? It doesn't matter if someone helped your girlfriend or a colleague. How can they help you? Don't give money to anyone without doing due diligence.

Outgrowing

The downside to growth is that sometimes you outgrow things and people. Not everyone will support you as your business evolves and grows. It's lonely at the top until you find the party. It's okay. They are not rejecting you. They are not even rejecting your ideas. People reject what they do not understand. Explaining yourself doesn't always help. The person who rejects you may need to get there on their own. That's fine. Be the one waiting for them at the top.

I remember the day I felt like I had outgrown my clothes. It was like staring into another person's closet. Another strange occurrence was the timing. It was the day my Admin to VA Summit ended. I thought I would feel relaxed or relief. I didn't. Instead I felt like I stepped into the next version of me. The version that doesn't wear these clothes.

If I were at home, I'm fairly certain things wouldn't have been so drastic. I wasn't at home though. I was in Morocco. My traveling-the-world wardrobe was not a true representation of how I felt or who I'd become. That day I went shopping and throughout the rest of the year, I shed my old wardrobe for what this new me wears.

The saying goes "Dress for the job you want, not the job you have." Well, I'm a VA matchmaker and consultant, an author, and now I was a summit host too. I don't have a job. I created my own career. In addition, I had become location independent.

For years, I've witnessed the same transition in others. It could be a bold new haircut, a stunning watch, signature shoes. I knew it was never about what the person was wearing; it was about how the person was owning the look. However, until now I didn't truly understand what was going on inside of me.

Others shed things instead of adding. Of course, we all know the famous Steve Jobs look. Some people leave the city and move to the country. There are movements of minimalism and tiny homes. Even though people are downsizing, they are still outgrowing something and making changes.

What or who have you outgrown? It certainly doesn't have to be your clothes. Could it be your mindset? Is it your level of clientele? Maybe you're outgrowing partners in the industry. Outgrowing things isn't bad. Be concerned if you are in business and never reach a point of outgrowing anything. If you aren't growing, you are getting passed up!

Growth can be both exciting and scary, especially when we feel like we've outgrown our former self. Dr. Ato (who I previously mentioned in chapter 3) says, "We're always outgrowing ourselves, but we're not always paying attention to it. What you are saying goodbye to are aspects of your life you no longer want to bring forth first. Moving through any change, loss or transition requires reintegration. Understanding how it's affecting you, how you want to get through it, and understanding if you are letting things go they aren't being thrown out into the universe orbiting somewhere. What you are letting go of is your attachment to them. They are always parts of you. The change is you're no longer leading with that as your identity."

When you truly outgrow your current situation, you'll know. Then the question becomes, what will you do about it? Dr. Ato says, "When making the leap, be deliberate in your trajectory. Ask yourself, 'How is this position going to help me get closer to my big life goals?' We usually get ourselves stuck in the worse case scenario. We tend to overinvest in our fear, rather than overinvesting in our faith."

How to Feed Your Faith and Starve Your Fears

Faith shouldn't just be reserved for religion. Faith simply is allegiance to a duty or a person. As a virtual assistant business owner, you have a duty to yourself. You are the person who also needs to have your faith.

I don't think there is anyone who doesn't understand fear. Fear is a word we not only use, but we choose our own adjectives. We go into much descriptive detail to describe it. In essence, we feed it.

Starting a business isn't all sunshine and rainbows. Or is it? Let's think about this for a moment. Rainbows come after the rain. If it were always raining, there would be a flood. However, if it never rained, there would be a drought. We need both sunshine and rain (to make the rainbows) in life and business.

The problem is we feed fear instead of faith. We ask Fear questions it can't answer, and often our questions aren't even probable. We get close to the edge, look over, and scare ourselves. We don't put up boundaries or fences and let Fear creep onto our property, and then we're startled when it knocks at the door. Life without fear is not realistic. Living in constant fear isn't healthy.

Remember those boundaries you set up at the beginning of your business? You need to revisit them as you grow. You're growing, which naturally implies stretching your borders. You might need more faith in one thing but less fear of something else. Either way, this requires yet another version of yourself.

You control your business actions. If you don't have enough clients, you can change that. If you're struggling with too many clients, you can implement changes to lessen the burden. If you need help, it's up to you to get it. Instead, what so many VAs do is sit in fear and wait. There is no greater food source for fear than inaction. Paralysis by fear means you have fed it and it has enough food to live on throughout the winter. Imagine if you fed your faith the same way.

Remember, to feed your faith is to feed your allegiance to yourself and your business. It's not an accident. Instead of getting a quick fix and drive-thru meals, which you know are bad for your health, plan a meal worthy of consumption, a meal that will fuel your body. Here's how to do it:

Start the morning off with the right energy.

Feed Your Faith: Notice I didn't say to start the morning with what makes you feel good. Ice cream makes me feel good. I could eat it every day. But it doesn't give me energy. Instead of eating ice cream in the morning, I exercise, read, and write. I read motivational daily emails from Marc and Angel Hack Life and TUT (Thoughts Become Things) to encourage and inspire me. When I open my laptop to start my day, I search for these messages first, before I respond to any other emails. It's amazing how much I look forward to these messages and the energy they give me.

Starve Your Fear: Quit doing the thing that gives you the most anxiety first thing every morning! I don't remember the last time I turned on a television in the morning. There was once a time when I watched the news every morning and kept it on in the background as I got ready for work and sent my children off to school. Only when I stopped doing this did I realize how much happier I was. No more awful horror stories or doom and gloom to start my days.

Schedule your perfect working day.

Feed Your Faith: Do the work. If you don't have any clients or enough clients to keep you busy, practice the work you would do for them. Reach out to your ideal clients. Take a free class. Learn something. Be diligent. Choose three things you'll do today to grow your business. Start connecting and reaching out to potential clients who can make it happen.

Starve Your Fear: Don't get dusty. When things aren't going well, we tend to let our schedules get away from us. This includes checking social media where you find all your friends having better lives than you. It must be true because they've got the photos to prove it, right? I'm always amazed when I ask struggling VAs what their days look like, and their schedules are scattered all over the place and they don't send outbound emails, don't make calls, and ultimately don't make any connections. Quit looking at other people's lives and start creating your own.

Hire a coach.

Feed Your Faith: Support and accountability are crucial. I'm not selling you anything, nor am I a coach so I don't benefit from telling you to hire someone. I'm telling you this because hiring the right coach can make all the difference in the world. You will experience countless benefits when you ask someone with a proven track record to help you uncover blind spots and challenge your perceptions while keeping you accountable.

Starve Your Fear: Instead of worrying if a coach will make a difference or not, think about how the coach *will* make a difference. Forget about the "or not." I didn't have the extra money to spend on my first coach, but I couldn't afford not to hire one either. Had I not hired her, who knows if I would even still be in business today.

Acknowledge your fear.

Feed Your Faith: Write down your fear and be honest. Don't add the what ifs or worst case scenarios. Then write down the solution to the fear, and the steps you should take to keep shrinking it until it's not something you think about every day. Not everything deserves your attention. Focus your attention on the faith of your actions.

Starve Your Fear: Recognize what your fear is and put up boundaries. Don't feed it. Don't pet it or play with it. Without boundaries, the closer it gets to you, the more you feed it. It was not meant to consume you or become part of your life like the family pet.

Fear is a part of life and can even be healthy. The problem is we not only feed it, but we overfeed it and let it bite off our hand in the process. What would your business look like if you spent as much time having faith in yourself and your actions as you spend time worrying? Success is not a place. It's a mindset. Have faith you will get there, and you will.

As you continue to grow and expand your business, you drill down deeper, peel back more layers of the onion. When growing outwardly, you'll find that the inner work becomes more intense and even harder at times. The reason is because as you grow your business the right way, you get to the core of yourself and your unique gifts, passions, and desires. You grow as a person. Growing outwardly without doing the inner work will not help you when you face difficult questions from clients or experience bumps in the road.

The process doesn't have to be a long, drawn out, "kumbaya" experience. My last instance of this was while speaking to a friend over Skype. We've never met, and I try to keep up with all my personal and close business contacts at least once a quarter. On my social media accounts, I post about what I'm doing. But to keep the relationships strong, I want to know what they are doing. My friend was in the middle of a rebranding and shared his story with me. His name is Dr. Alvin C. Miles, and he teaches mid-career professionals how to advance to the next level in their careers.

As he began to share how he coaches and the funnel process of breaking down his practice, he asked me rhetorically, "Could you imagine if you didn't know your gift was communication?" Huh? I tried not to act surprised, as if I did know already. But I didn't. What he was saying made sense. It's a fundamental business practice and the basis for how I match clients to VAs. Additionally, I write. A lot. Oddly enough, I didn't see that as a form of communicating.

With this newfound information given to me, which was so painfully obvious, I had to ask myself how I could have overlooked it for so long. The answer came quickly. While I struggled through 15 years of marriage, I read every book I could get my hands on about marriage and communicating with your spouse. I went to conferences and seminars. I devoured information on communicating.

In between the marriage books, I read books on how to communicate with your children. From toddlers, to adolescents, to teens and young adults, I consumed it all. However, since this was all long before I ever decided to start my own company, I didn't make the connection. Honestly, I had forgotten how much time I spent reading about communication in my personal life. Instead I went back into my work life to search for clues on what I'm good at and why.

This is the place where I am now. Between writing this book and releasing it, I discovered even more about myself. By the time you finish reading this book, you will have discovered more about yourself too.

Summary

Growing Your Business

- To achieve—and more importantly to receive—from growing your business, make sure it is ready and primed for success. You can get what your heart desires, but if it comes at the wrong time or all at once, you have to be prepared if you plan on enjoying it.

- Ask yourself the right questions even when you don't have the answers. They'll never come if you don't. Monthly check-ins with yourself are crucial to stay on track.

- Client referrals and gifting are an essential part of growing your business and continuing to attract your ideal clients. This is the best way to grow your business using your dollars wisely and building a quality reputation.

- You don't need another you. You need someone to complement and support you. Know when it's time to hire support and know it doesn't have to be business related.

- Reevaluate your success measures. If you have changed and grown, your ideal client has too. Be ready to hire a business coach to help take you to the next level.

Marketing

- Remember, getting out of your comfort zone is uncomfortable not painful. If you are finding marketing more than uncomfortable, something is wrong.

- There are many different marketing strategies. Know which strategy is right for you and make sure you're taking advice from the right person. Your business isn't one size fits all. Your marketing plan can't be either.

- While growing your business and certainly while marketing it, you may find that you've outgrown people and the old version of yourself. That's okay. Growth is natural and part of the experience. In the form of growth, change can be painful but it doesn't have to be if you can say goodbye properly to your former self and know she hasn't gone away. She's just not appearing daily any longer.

- It can be scary to become more successful and step into the truest version of yourself. You might find yourself in uncomfortable territory. Know which steps to take to feed your faith and starve your fears.

Growing and marketing your business aren't simply functional processes. They're emotional ones. High achievers struggle just like everyone else because we push ourselves to the limit seeing our dreams on the other side. Be prepared to do the inner work, not simply the outer work.

In the next chapter, we'll discuss your clients' ever-changing needs as well as technology. What is all the rage today can quickly become obsolete next month or next year. This is why I purposefully wrote this chapter last. Additionally, depending on the type of VA you are, your clients' needs and technology will vary greatly. More than anything, it's about staying informed and knowing what is changing before it's too late.

CHAPTER 8

Step 8: Client Needs and Technology

"A true pilot studies his craft in every season, all that concerns his art."

—Plato

Determining what your clients need is a learning process, one which can be accomplished through networking, asking, and even surveys. People don't like to complete surveys, so don't bank on this. Asking other VAs in the field will definitely point you in the right direction.

Depending on which field you begin in, there will be no shortage of software and technology to learn. Keep in mind you can learn many for free and directly from the source. Companies want you to use their software. Believe me when I say they are happy to chat with you on the benefits of using their software—what it can do, the new features coming out soon. Keep up with which technologies integrate well together and which ones don't.

There are some basics you should begin with. No matter what type of client you are serving, it is likely both of you need an appointment scheduling tool, a video chat system, a way to send newsletters and email marketing/drip campaigns, a file-sharing system, and a CRM (customer relationship management system). In the Resources section, I've listed some of the most common options in the industry. However, keep in mind what is most common may not be the best choice for you or your clients.

Research your clients and anticipate their needs before they verbalize them. Know which software best fits their needs and budget. Many software options are free to begin with or at least have a free version with fewer options. This is part of your professional development. As an admin, I'm sure you are no stranger to professional development. You may even enjoy taking classes for fun. This is both an advantage and a disadvantage. I want to remind you that you're not perfect and you can't be. You can't know everything about everything.

Why do I tell you this? Because I see virtual assistants often get trapped in this stage. They don't offer their services because they're not the best. They're afraid someone is going to ask them to do something they can't do even though they can find the answer. They're not worried about not figuring it out. They're worried about how to charge for something they don't know how to do yet.

A few things to keep in mind:

- Don't charge for your time to learn.

- Be upfront and confident about your skills simultaneously.

- Set your fee for what you would charge if this wasn't your first time.

How do you figure out that last one? Ask the company that produces the software or technology. One of the reasons I was so valuable as an EA is because I always went straight to the source. I was and am still very low-tech. I hate apps. I don't enjoy online research. I'd rather pick up the phone and ask my question to someone who can answer it. So that's what I do. Instead of exchanging numerous emails back and forth, I ask my questions in real time, and in the process I learn how to easily get answers to my future questions.

Some companies do not offer customer service over the phone, but they usually have pretty good online customer support. If not, you should seriously consider whether or not you want to work with them. Again, ask people in your network what they do when they run into issues with specific technology. You even can ask them about how much time a certain project should take.

Part of gathering information is to continuously stay up to date and to keep abreast of the latest and greatest. However, there is a point where it becomes too much. You can only take in so much information. How do you know when enough is enough? When you are learning things you never use and cannot retain. Here are few tips:

- Get your information curated. Not only does this put everything in one spot, but the curator is usually not biased, so you can get the pros and cons of multiple products at one single time.

- Use trusted sources. Don't read and listen to everyone. They will contradict one another. Find the sources that are easy to read, bookmark, search, and—most importantly—helpful. Trust those sources and follow them.

- Set aside a training day. Don't simply learn information. Put it to the test. Schedule time to see if it works how you thought it should. Is it as simple as it sounds? Make sure there aren't any missing steps.

What about technology that phases out assistants, like artificial intelligence? There are two sides to every coin. Not all intelligence is artificial, and not all artificial computers and robots are intelligent. Think about how you can use them to your advantage. You have two distinct advantages to artificial intelligence—you have the common sense and a sense of humor that artificial intelligence lacks.

There once was a special episode of "Gilligan's Island" where the Harlem Globetrotters played a basketball game against robots. (Don't ask.) The Globetrotters were losing the game badly, even though they were considered the best. However, when they did the exact things that made them the Globetrotters, they won the game. What did they do? Their tricks, gimmicks, and fun maneuvers.

As technology advances, the fear remains the same. People in all fields fear losing their jobs because of technology. It's only half true. Even by the year 2075, it's estimated that 45 percent of current jobs will be obsolete. That's just under half. However, ten years ago we couldn't have predicted the jobs we have now, and we can't predict the jobs of the future. Work with what you know and play up to your strengths. Don't fight technology. Figure out how you can partner with it. Find the win-win.

Some of your clients' needs may be best served by artificial intelligence. These are the jobs you don't even want to do because they will take up too much of your time without providing any satisfaction. It's part of the reason chatbots were invented. What if your business as a VA was to help clients with chatbots?

Client needs and technology are constantly changing. Your job is to keep on top of these changes. Know what is a fad, when it's time to switch and migrate, and when old-fashioned has become new again. This is what makes you invaluable to your clients. This is what makes you better than a robot.

As a virtual assistant, you need to know your competition intimately. No longer is your competition solely another human being or VAs in low-cost countries. Now we are competing against artificial intelligence, the same AI that makes our own lives easier. Virtual assistants must embrace technology while being responsible with boundaries and expectations, looking after the quality of life for those we support. This means that you have to work on this as well.

So how do you compete with bots?

- Know which bots are good for your clients and which aren't. Not all bots are created equal. Throwing away all options isn't an option.

- Prepare your research so you're always ready to speak to your clients. It's not solely on the basis of productivity and efficiency. We're talking about the quality of a person's life. Just because you can do something all the time doesn't mean you should.

- Discuss bots that are available and how they fit into your clients' plans for having assistance available when you're not. Consider bots as a collaborative partner.

- Don't be afraid to ask the tough questions or say what needs to be said. Your clients' health could very well be at risk.

- Never underestimate the power of having your clients know you don't just work for them, you *enjoy* working for them. Tell them how much pleasure your work brings you. Since a bot doesn't have real feelings, it can't reciprocate in the same way.

Technology is always changing. You won't be able to stop all advancements, and that isn't the point. What you need to do is educate yourself and understand your competition. Especially learn the advantages you have over technology and how those advantages benefit your clients and yourself.

Is Your Planning Coming at the Expense of Your Productivity?

I love planning. My office is literally covered in calendars. I have written all kinds of events, meetings, telephone calls, and vacation days on these calendars. They are a constant visual reminder to me of how busy I am, how much free time I have, how I shouldn't spread myself too thin, and when I need to pick up my pace.

Then there is overplanning, those subtle ways we try to trick ourselves into believing we're being productive with our planning when we're not. Do you find yourself doing any of the following?

- **Planning to the point of procrastination.** In your mind, you are aware that as long as you keep planning, you don't have to take action. Planning is merely the pathway. Action is what will take you to the desired location. The sooner you start the journey, the sooner you'll arrive at the destination.

- **Planning for perfection.** Having a Plan B is good. Having a Plan C, D, and E is too much. Find this habit hard to break? To successfully change this behavior, think of a way to hand over the reins or at least share them with someone else. Chances are, if you're a perfectionist, you are a people-pleaser as well. If you have to share responsibilities with someone else and they say you are driving them crazy, you'll be more likely to change your behavior. Another tip is to do something with your creative mind instead of your analytical mind. Art is a great way to find beauty *in* the imperfections.

- **Planning because you're afraid.** You tell yourself you're preparing for the future, while what you're really doing is planning for the worst. This is not a good use of your time. The future is rarely as bad as we make it out to be, and some of the things that we call "bad" actually turn out to be the best blessings.

In April 2015, I was fortunate enough to attend HustleCon, a conference for non-technical startups. I heard from many great founders who spoke about the early days of their companies. They shared about the problems they faced, the daily struggles, the financial setbacks, the failed attempts, and the constant changing of their circumstances.

The founder that had the biggest impact on me was Andrew Warner of Mixergy. At that time in his life, he was speaking about already achieving success and selling his company. Now he was trying something new and was feeling overwhelmed by how he envisioned the future.

During his travels, he came across a focus bead bracelet. He used the bracelet to focus his energy and to keep things in perspective. He didn't need a million followers. At the time Andrew just wanted to get to 200. Whenever he got sidetracked or overwhelmed, he held the beads and ran his fingers over each one, repeating to himself that he was on his way to 200—200 was possible.

Maybe you don't struggle with overplanning. What is stopping you from being productive? For many of us, the very thing that we're so good at also stands in our way to success. If you're a chef, do you keep adding ingredients to the plate? If you're a painter, do you keep painting long after your artwork is complete? If you're a speaker, do you keep talking even though no one is listening? If you're in sales, do you keep trying to sell to someone who isn't buying when the next customer is actually ready to buy?

Whether you use focus beads, the Serenity Prayer, a quick pep talk to yourself, or something else, take a moment to stop when you feel yourself overwhelmed and the pressure is rising. Being productive doesn't mean you hit the goal today. It's taking action to get that much closer to it.

Summary

- Client needs and the technology you'll use will vary depending on each of your clients. Be sure to review the Resources page for what every client will (or at least should be) using as a foundational tool. Your clients don't have to use any of these, but chances are they will. Do your research to discover the options that best fit not only your clients' needs but their budget as well.

- Researching, planning, and learning are great until they affect your productivity. At some point you have to make the leap and experiment with what you know. Be honest, transparent and—most importantly—know how to get immediate help and support.

I've included a bonus section for those of you who have yet to go out on your own as a VA. (Although a lot will still be useful for anyone who is already a VA.) Whether you are ready to leave your current position now or have a plan to exit in the future, you can definitely start preparing using the information in this bonus section.

BONUS—BEFORE YOU
GO OUT ON YOUR OWN

What Is the Future of Executive Assistants?

In the age of bots and artificial intelligence, some might say that no job is safe. I agree. Whether or not technology advances are purposely trying to eliminate jobs, it's happening. One industry advances while another slowly becomes obsolete. Could executive assistants be next?

In Deloitte's 2016 Millennial Survey, the company addressed how millennials no longer should be seen as the leaders of tomorrow but as the leaders of today. Seventy-five percent of those leaders have a desire for freedom, flexibility, and location independence.

The majority of research says that by 2020, 50 percent of the entire workforce will be remote. Statistics of companies increasing their remote workforce have also steadily risen and are projected to continue rising in the coming years. (You can read some of the latest studies at Global Workplace Analytics.)

Don't think it can happen to executive assistants? Ask a journalist. Research the diminishing sales of print advertisers.

Look at the similarities between journalists and executive assistants:

- Companies need skilled assistants. American citizens need experienced, trained journalists.

- When companies don't use skilled assistants, the companies run inefficiently. When news organizations lack true journalists, Americans cannot get accurate facts and informative news.

- Companies are hiring unskilled talent or replacing admins with bots and apps. Americans are being fooled and fed lies by anyone with access to the internet.

- The need for companies and business owners to have highly trained assistants has never been greater. The need to separate truth from lies and signal from the noise has never been greater.

So what can you learn from the journalism field to save your own job? Well, to start, you can't ignore the signs. The job growth rate for an assistant is -5 percent between 2016 and 2026. With the rate at which technology is advancing, I believe this number will rise. Only a year ago the growth rate was at 3 percent. Now it's negative! That's saying a lot, considering that the growth rate was already lower than average.

Many journalists became freelancers as the digital industry became the preferred source of information. How can you use your skills in the digital era? Many executive assistants will say their greatest skill is what they bring in person to the office and the person they support, a skill that doesn't translate online. You must be able to define your skills beyond a physical presence.

Is this the beginning of the end for the executive assistant? As we know the position now, yes. Are our careers over? No. However, the past already tells us that business is not performing as usual. Executive assistants need to do what we've always done—change and grow with the times. Think you're safe because your company couldn't do without you? Do they know what to do with you as they hire more remote workers? Do you know how to support executives remotely? Any industry that believes this can't happen to them is at the most risk.

We, as admins, cannot afford to get comfortable. There's no need to be anxious either. Those of us who have the calling will make the way. Don't wait for what you know is coming to make a change and start down this path. "The future belongs to those who prepare for it today," so start by paving your future career path.

Why All Admins Should Have Something on the Side

No matter if you plan to become a VA or not, it is important to have something on the side. You might call it a side hustle, a passion project, or a hobby. Whatever the case, this is the opportunity to hone your skills, make contacts, and use an entirely different set of skills. In fact, it was my passion project that started it all, and I didn't even realize I had been a virtual assistant because I enjoyed doing what I loved that much!

One of my great loves is the sport of wrestling (not WWE!). I remember being on a long drive with my son and talking. I asked him a question about his plans for the future. What would be his absolute dream job without putting any restrictions on it? He then asked me the same question. Without hesitation my response was "Work for the Virginia Tech wrestling team." He laughed and asked what in the world I would do for them. I reminded him there were no restrictions.

A few years later, I received an email from the head coach. It was the team's monthly newsletter. In his message, he stated he was running behind schedule and apologized for sending the newsletter out late. He mentioned not having an assistant, and my mind was blown. How was he getting everything done? How was he supposed to be a coach and his own administrative assistant? I responded to the email with my sincere concern for his lack of administrative support. I told him that if I lived closer, I would have been happy to volunteer, but I was moving back to California the next day.

Within a few hours, the coach responded with another email message. He was convinced I could do what he needed from anywhere and asked if I was interested. I was! That was actually my first virtual assistant position, and I considered it an internship. I had no idea at the time that email exchange would turn into something more, that I would eventually work as a VA for him and live out my dreams. And I certainly didn't expect to sign a contract for over $20,000 for doing something I was willing to do for free.

Not only does your passion project hone your skills and help you improve your time management, the contacts and connections you can leverage are extremely valuable.

Diana Brandl is a great example of turning a passion project into a business. I had the pleasure of meeting Diana in Berlin during my travels abroad in July of 2017. We were connected through a mutual group, OfficeNinjas. At the time, Diana was the senior executive assistant for Mister Spex, an online eyewear retailer based in Europe. Her passion project was writing her own blog called The Socialista Projects. She even began influencing the blogging industry with her creative initiatives. One of those initiatives is launching the hashtag #WeAreInThisTogether.

Through her blog, initiatives, and commitment to organizations such as International Management Assistants (IMA), Diana is now an international speaker and writes for multiple publications in her homeland of Germany and abroad.

In just a year, Diana's blog has come a long way, and she maintains such a busy schedule. I wondered what made her commit to doing it. Diana said, "I have always enjoyed writing, and I felt it was time to share a few stories with my network. I am a true storyteller and see this blog as an open book for my community. They meet fellow assistants, read their stories in my interviews and simply get inspired by the activities I launch there, such as #WeAreInThisTogether."

Diana's story is aligned with her passions, abilities, talents, and skills. It's not surprising to me that she has grown an organic following of professionals in Europe, South Africa, Canada, the United States, and many other countries.

When Diana first started blogging, she didn't expect to receive much interest from her readers. She said, "Of course, there is always room for improvement, but I am super happy how this blog developed in the meantime. I have a great fan base of followers, and they motivate me to continue this work although it costs so much extra time. It goes without saying that this blog helped me in my visibility. I can share my work there and promote all my activities as well."

This visibility now allows her to travel the world, speaking and doing what she loves. However, when I first met Diana, it seemed she could never imagine not working in an office. I wondered what had changed. Her response, "Although I had all these ideas already in my head when I met you, I was just not ready to say it out loud. I had a fantastic job, amazing bosses, and many great projects—so it was the best timing ever to follow my own vision now. I realized that I have reached everything I ever wanted in my professional life as an executive assistant, including holding a senior title, working as a team lead, and leading many important projects. I knew that no other employer would top this. I had to top it myself with my own dream. And I dreamt of it for a while."

It may be scary to think about your passion project or doing something on the side before you go out on your own because either of these opportunities will take away some of your free time. That's why you should only invest your time in what you love. While right now it's uncertain whether you'll generate income from your passion later, the experience now is extremely valuable. Plus, the unexpected benefits you reap are the best surprises!

How to Intern Properly

I've decided to cover internships in the bonus section because they are typically unpaid. However, they can be extremely valuable when done right. Again, look for the win-win situation. This isn't just about the other person getting you to work for free. You are learning a skill, a mindset, a business model, and more, all in exchange for a referral—and you're only doing the work for a specific amount of time.

My internship with VT Wrestling was only unpaid for one year—my first year. My second year I was paid, and by the third year I was compensated at a level I had never imagined was possible, even for my dream job. However, it wasn't only about the work or the money. Not even the love of it. I was learning from the coach, and I watched how he conducted business, how he raised funds, how he dealt with people, and answered the tough questions. I quickly came to realize he wasn't the head coach because he couldn't do anything else. He did so because he loved it. He could have been the CEO of any company because he knew how to monetize, how to attract the best talent, how to delegate and outsource, and how not to micromanage anyone.

When you are thinking about asking for or accepting an internship, follow these guidelines:

Reasons to do an internship:

- Because you don't have practical applications yet.

- You are new to the field.

- To be able to offer an additional service(s).

Knowledge you should have already:

- **Basic knowledge of the field.** You wouldn't hire a legal intern who wasn't already going to law school. The amount of knowledge you have may vary; however, this is what you are studying and training for.

- **A minimum amount of training.** The internship is providing *additional* training. The company or individual should not be training you from scratch. An internship isn't merely a training course. It is an application scenario. Yes, you will have questions that your mentor can answer, but they should be thoughtful questions.

- **The benefit you are looking to receive.** Internships are to benefit the intern. The company does benefit in the long run because it possibly can hire you in the future. You never intern for a company who is simply wanting to get work done for free.

How long is an internship?

- Depending on the company, an internship can be anywhere from one week to 12 months. I suggest that you agree to a firm end date at the very beginning of your internship.

- Ideally, you should have a three-month internship. A shorter internship means you haven't gone through a full quarter cycle, and a longer internship could mean that the relationship will begin to sour. Keep in mind, this a two-fold benefit.

A few important guidelines:

- No one can set the hours you work. They must be mutually agreed upon.

- No one can provide equipment, hardware, or software to you.

- In many cases, not paying an intern is illegal. Be very careful to follow the appropriate federal guidelines.

What are some additional benefits?

- You will receive free advice from coaches and consultants.

- You will receive introductions to your mentor's network upon the satisfactory completion of the internship.

- You will receive opportunities to participate in meetings where you will gain further insight into how your potential clients are thinking and what they are concerned about.

- You will receive mentoring and real-time training. The time you spend in daily and weekly conversations should provide feedback and coaching on how you will work with clients just like them.

- You should receive a glowing referral from the company upon the successful completion of the internship.

Which companies typically fall into the category of being a good match for an intern?

Typically, the right company or individual falls into **all** of the following categories:

- A company that is operating in its first year of business.

- A company that is bootstrapping its business and not covering all of its expenses yet.

- A company that has time to write a policy and/or an SOP (standard operating procedures manual). You, as the intern, should not be expected to complete this.

- A mentor who enjoys training others and can dedicate the appropriate time to that training.

If the company falls into these categories, follow these next steps:

1. **Decide on a single three-month project**. The project can incorporate several duties or tasks, but they all should have a direct correlation to the final outcome.

2. **Determine the benefits**. What will you walk away with after three months that you can charge a client for in the future?

3. **Consider the time commitment.** How much time are you expected to devote every week to your internship? It should be no more than 10 hours (on the high side) per week, including meetings and mentoring.

4. **Determine if this is your ideal client.** If not, do not accept the position. You only want to work with your ideal clients. It's hard enough working for no pay when you love the work and the company. If you don't like the company or the client, it can be your worst nightmare.

5. **Don't accept an internship that asks for free work or samples of your work upfront**. The company is already asking too much of you. Plus, remember this is an internship to help you gain experience.

How to Leverage Your Current Contacts

Since admins are most commonly givers, it can often be uncomfortable for us to ask for help and guidance. It almost feels like sales. Here's the thing—people actually want to help you. They just don't know how. When we do make our ask, it can be too vague or on the opposite end of the spectrum of an ask. You need to find the space that is a win-win for both parties. The win could simply be that the other party feels good to have helped you.

The best source for help is your current contacts. Leveraging your contacts can be done in a variety of ways. You can volunteer, join a board, ask someone to look over your online profile, or ask someone to introduce you to a contact in their network. Don't be afraid to ask for references and recommendations before you need them. Only ask people who really know you, and be prepared when they suggest that you write your own recommendation and allow them to edit it. As always, be specific.

Maybe your side hustle is a blog or a podcast. Consider interviewing people in your contacts for your next podcast or ask your writer contacts to be guest bloggers. While leveraging your current contacts, you're actually building up your online profile. And your online profile is the one that matters most as a VA.

Remember Diana Brandl? She was leveraging her contacts and associations. She holds a degree in international administration and management, specializing in office management. Throughout her career, she has worked successfully for C-level executives within global corporations. However, all this would have taken Diana only so far if not for her strong background in communications and her efforts as an active networker.

Diana joined the professional network International Management Assistants (IMA) in 2006 and is a member of the board, serving as acting public relations officer for IMA Germany. When I asked her why she joined IMA, here's what she shared: "A colleague brought me to IMA. She took me to one of their regional events, and I was immediately motivated to join, so it did not take long until I wrote my application. I had no idea about networking at that time, but IMA opened the door to this area. I was basically trained to be a networker and ambassador of this profession by IMA."

Networking is great, but will only take you so far. What you give is what you get. I wondered what made Diana take an active role in IMA. "Once I moved from the south of Germany to Berlin, I decided to take the opportunity to take over the Berlin Regional Group, which was at that time led by a lady who lived in a different region in Germany. So it was hard for her to manage the group by being away. I saw this wonderful opportunity in finding new IMA friends in Berlin and of course taking over an active role as regional head. Lucky me as it was just the right function for me. I led the group for a few years, then stepped down (although involved all the time), and then took over the role again as there was nobody who would do it. I am also national press relations officer (acting) of IMA Germany at the moment. Lots of extra work—but so worth it!"

It's obvious that IMA has had a great impact on Diana's present and past career paths. In her own words, "It is a huge part of my life. Once I decide to dedicate myself to a project, I do it 100 percent, which means going many extra miles and trying to juggle my job, my family, and the work for IMA. Over the years, IMA brought new friends into my life, I learned many new perspectives on how to work together, and I simply learned a lot out of the conferences and seminars I attended. I brought back to my working environment lots of knowledge and expertise that I gained through IMA. However, working in such associations also means that there are many egos that come together, which sometimes doesn't make it easy to work on your goals. But this also helps me in growing, and I am thankful for such lessons learned."

It was extremely evident to me that making personal connections is important to Diana. She not only was eager to make time to meet with me but do so on a Monday! I appreciated her thoughtfulness in having the room set up with water and snacks and the attention to detail of even the choice of water, sparkling or still. Does she consider herself an introvert or an extrovert? I thought I knew, but I wanted to hear it from Diana: "Definitely an extrovert."

No matter if you consider yourself an introvert or an extrovert, Diana's advice still holds true. "I would probably not be as far as I am right now without the right network. The right community is crucial when you walk new paths. I have always been a strong networker, and I was there helping others. It is just wonderful to see how this network now helps me growing in my new role. I will be forever thankful. So make sure that there is a solid base before you work on such ideas. Your community can be your next customers—never forget."

Diana's career path is her own, but you may find many commonalties along your path. She stepped out of one career and straight into another with a smooth transition. Yet, there is something she wished she would have done differently. "I should have taken some time off. I stepped out of a full-time position in September 2017 and did not expect to be so busy until the end of the year—which is of course fantastic. I have been busy speaking and teaching as well as working as an interim assistant here and there. Plus, all the writing I do in the background. I truly wanted to enjoy the rest of 2017 and start strong in 2018, but once there is interest in your work, you have to grab the chance. And I did."

Diana's advice to a current admin considering going out on their own is, "Have a clear vision, goals, and a roadmap. Strategy behind such adventures is everything, so talk to many people about your idea and reach out to your network. Helping hands and lots of advice is never enough. And trust your gut feeling. Because a well prepared business plan will not make you happy when you feel that something is missing. Talk to your network and see how others have created their businesses. Best practice sharing is essential."

How to Ask Your Employer to Go Remote

What if you're not ready to go out on your yet? What if you just want to try working outside of the office? Great! Ask your employer about the option of working from home a few days a week or even full-time. I was fortunate, when I left my last in-office position, that my employer was so forward-thinking. Even though I had already been acting as a VA, I didn't realize it. I did have to prepare a proposal for working from home. Depending on your place of employment, a formal proposal may be required as well. As you create your proposal, put yourself in your boss's position. Think like he or she thinks so you can be prepared to answer questions as they come up.

Do your homework and gather your research to prepare a quality proposal. Begin by keeping track of how often you are required to work in person. Not how often people get ahold of you because you're in the office but because you could not physically address the issue if you were not in the office. It's usually less time than you think. I guarantee your employer has no idea. It is comforting when your boss sees you at your desk—even if you don't have enough work to keep you busy, or you have finished all of your tasks and are looking for more things to do.

Create a written proposal. The more business-minded you can be, the more business-minded and less emotional your boss will be. You want to take emotion out of the decision because your boss's emotion most likely will be fear—fear of not having you in the office, fear that you won't complete your work, fear of things falling through the cracks. The more professional you can be about the ask, the more your request will be considered.

Investigate how you will work from home. Which hardware and software will your employer need to provide to you? How much will it cost? What will your company receive in return for your working remotely?

Some people have a very easy time asking to work from home, and some companies don't require such diligent research and formal written pro-posals. A participant in my online class, The Essential Business Model for VAs, simply approached her boss and said she needed to go remote or she would have to quit. Now, this approach is a bit extreme, but it wasn't a bluff. She was prepared either way. Her family had already discussed the situation and was ready for either decision. Her employer agreed to her proposal, and within weeks she had become a remote employee. The time and cost to hire and train her replacement would have been too great.

Setting a New Work Schedule

When I worked in traditional offices with traditional business hours, I learned how to schedule my days to be the most productive. I created a system so no matter which emergencies or crises came my way, I could handle them and still accomplish what needed to get done.

Thinking back to my first week of working from home, I had no problems to fix and no interruptions, and yet I was completely unproductive. I was trying to keep regular business hours when I didn't have to. I had this new freedom and was still confining myself to my old schedule. The adrenaline rushes that used to come from putting out fires and would push me to get some of the more undesirable tasks done no longer existed. Even the simple things like getting dressed in my "work" clothes and doing my hair and makeup made the day awful. Now I found myself all dressed up with nowhere to go.

During my second week as a remote employee, I made the necessary changes to ensure I could be productive while working from home. As a virtual assistant, creating a home strategy is important. You may struggle to be productive because you're used to being constantly busy. The downtime can be confusing. Some VAs find that they feel guilty when spending time with their families because they know there is still work to be done. Or there may be a great demand in your work, yet you go the entire day and don't feel like you really accomplished anything. Here are some tips for you:

1. **Take an assessment of what makes you *feel* productive.** What is productive and what makes you feel productive may not always be the same thing. If you can start the day by doing things that make you feel productive, you'll end the day just as strong. Days when you don't feel or truly aren't productive rarely mean you did less work.

2. **Be honest about which tasks will take more time to accomplish and which tasks you are simply procrastinating to do.** No matter who you are or what line of work you're in, procrastination is your worst enemy. Make plans to remove distractions when working on the projects that you usually procrastinate accomplishing. You will naturally let anything distract you. So close all of your browser tabs, set your phone to "do not disturb," and try working in a place where you'll want to finish your work and leave. Another option is to consider how much you'd be willing to pay someone else to do the task then outsource it.

3. **Break your day into blocks of time that fit your work and life.** I've had to change my schedule often in the past few years. I will continue to do so moving forward because my life is in a constant state of change. The key is knowing when you are at your best to do your best work for yourself and your clients. Depending on where in the world I am, this could be in the morning or in the middle of the night. Things haven't always worked out how I planned. There is always a learning curve when trying something new. The point is you have permission to change your schedule as needed and do what best suits you and your lifestyle.

4. **Review how you're going to spend your time every quarter.** Even the smallest changes can make a difference in your daily routine. The weather and time changes have an impact on me as a

"fair weather" runner. Something more significant, like conference season, needs to be worked out well before you begin. When I traveled the world in 2017, I set my goals based on the time zones I was in. I did my best to frontload those goals because the end of the year is busy enough. While it all looked good on paper, I wasn't planning for the fact that I'm a morning person who would be working graveyard shift hours. I thought if it was "technically" my morning, it would feel like morning. I was wrong. I was able to adjust by working the daylight hours on my own work and doing client work when the sun was down. I've learned my lesson for the future. I can do client work but not creative work on the graveyard shift.

5. **Don't be afraid to do what is right for you.** So many times, I've read about the person who wakes up at 5 a.m. to go to the gym, arrives at the office by 7 a.m., attends meetings until noon, and so on. That doesn't work for me. No matter how successful they are and no matter how much I would like to be as successful as them, I can't copy that schedule. Instead of forcing someone else's routine on yourself, spend your time learning their best business principles or their thought process and then apply those to your own schedule.

Freedom to work at your own pace is great. If this is a new concept for you, it can be overwhelming. Whatever you do should feel natural and be easily applied to your daily routine. If you can make it a part of your routine, you'll be more likely to stay consistent. If you're not consistent, you don't have a system that works. You are first a virtual assistant to yourself. If you can't help yourself, you can't help your clients.

You need to have a flow zone. Flow is the space of your greatest work, the kind that seems to be free flowing. Maybe you call it "being in the zone." Imagine for a moment you are an artist. For days you've stared at a blank canvas until it seems so clear, and then the brush strokes begin to fly as you create your next masterpiece. That is flow. Chances are you know what this looks like for your former bosses and your current clients. Now it's time to achieve this for yourself.

Where Is Your Best Place to Work?

Dr. Ron Friedman's book *The Best Place to Work* is an absolute must-read no matter where you work or for whom you work. Dr. Friedman addresses the science behind what makes a great place to work. He also gives insight into things we think are bad or even toxic, like gossip. Seriously, read his book.

I especially appreciated learning the science of why employees who work from home are often more productive than those in the office. There is no shortage of discussion about how working from home is more convenient. However, having a convenient workspace doesn't necessarily equal a productive employee.

As virtual assistants, the most common stereotype applied to us is that we have small children at home, so that's why we do what we do. While for some this might be true, most of the VAs I know don't have small children at home. In fact, when my kids were younger, I couldn't have worked at home because the distractions would have been too great.

It's no longer just virtual assistants either. Now just about any position can provide assistance virtually. And remote workspaces also are getting better. In April 2016, I had my first stay in a new kind of co-working and co-living space through Outsite. It's an entirely new way of working, providing networking opportunities and meaningful, creative collaborations.

The space was beautiful—a beachside villa in Santa Cruz, California. Outsite provided WiFi, coffee, tea, and collaborative spaces as you might imagine. However, it was also equipped with a yoga room, bicycles, beach gear, and weekly activities to participate in, like hiking, barbecues, and movie nights.

So where's my best place to work? I used to say, "Wherever I am." Some days that's at home. Other days it could be a coffee shop, a co-working space, a park bench, or even on an airplane 30,000 feet in the air. Working on the beach or poolside used to be a personal favorite.

As I traveled the world, I no longer use the same expression. Now I say, "Whatever space I create." Not all cities in the countries I visited are conducive to remote working. Internet connections aren't always great, plus what I can do and enjoy when I'm not working became a huge factor.

Am I still productive? You'd better believe I am! Instead of looking at posters of a beautiful place with a great quote, I'm at a beautiful place and don't need to be inspired by a quote. Are my clients able to reach me? Of course! My space reflects the work I'm accomplishing, and I also take into consideration what, if any, interruptions I can allow.

When I know I'll have a day with a lot of phone calls, I don't work in a coffee shop or anyplace where my conversations can be heard. When I need to bounce ideas off of someone or learn what another person's best practice is, collaborative spaces are great. Reading, editing, and writing were once done outside at the park, at the beach, or at another relaxing venue. But now I find myself far too distracted in these places and choose to stay in a quiet place instead.

As a virtual assistant, it is important to know your best place to work. You might need to take the time and energy to create that space in your home. Be careful to recognize when your perfect place changes. There was once a time I thought my ideal location was at the beach, but not all beaches are the same. And the beach for me simply meant overlooking the beach—not literally in the sand.

Whenever I feel myself on the verge of procrastination, I know I need to get to a place where I don't want to spend my hours and would feel like my time is wasted the longer I stayed. On these days, I have to get out of my house. Days full of phone conversations give me energy, and I find myself rejuvenated. I have to write in a quiet place, locked away from the rest of the world. But I do my best editing in an open space where I have enough quiet time to think but not space to overthink.

If you find that working from home is your only option, find or create nooks in your space. Make each space relevant and meaningful, conducive to your style of working.

When Is It Time to Ditch Being Virtual?

I'm so very thankful for virtual opportunities—opportunities to work, network, stay in touch with family and friends, even meet new people, all done virtually. Sometimes you need to get out IRL (in real life) though.

In October 2015, I had the opportunity and honor to host OfficeNinjas IRL in Dallas. No virtual casting could have taken the place of this live event. Hosting or not, being with over 300 administrative professionals from different companies with different administrative styles and backgrounds was amazing.

I got to meet a finalist for the Dallas Admin Awards in the Spirit category and the co-worker who nominated her. I met another woman who works as the sole administrative employee in her company.

I also was thrilled to be a part of the giveaways. Calling out names, then watching women run up to claim their prizes and have their photos taken was such a rush. I was hugging each winner, and I'm not a hugger. Then there were the moments I got to meet people I have been in the same online communities with for over a year, face to face, for the very first time. For all this I happily ditched being virtual!

Hopefully, you have already taken steps to join an in-person networking group. A good co-working space might also be a good way to keep company with fellow entrepreneurs. I have a love-hate relationship with co-working spaces. They are not all equal, and the projects I'm working on aren't always conducive to a co-working space. Some spaces have been absolutely wonderful for working, networking, learning, and general company. You have to be mindful of how much time you're spending alone (as in feeling it's just you against the world), without the company of your peers, or doing something you love.

Look for opportunities to meet clients in person, attend a conference or an in-person class. No matter how much I love and appreciate being virtual, human contact is necessary and fun! It takes some planning and creativity, and you could even be nervous at the prospect at first. However, this is also how opportunities are revealed.

This might be an exciting time for you to go out on your own. It could very well be a stressful time after being fired, laid off, or retiring before you were ready. There is power in saying goodbye. Dr. Ato explains, "These are rites of passages, like retirement and birthdays, worthy of acknowledgment."

In my own experience, it took me a long time to say goodbye properly. Virtual assistance wasn't the life or the career I had dreamed of. Instead I felt like it was forced upon me. I can look back now with warm, happy thoughts, but at the time I was scared. It wasn't just me—I had to provide for my family. Dr. Ato suggests that we "Bring our families through the process. Include them because there will be a ripple effect." Whether it is to discuss finances or talk about what your career change will mean to the entire family, "It is opening up dialogue to let others know it's okay to have feelings about the situation as well."

While you're saying goodbye to your old life, it is important to take proper care of yourself. Dr. Ato has practiced self-care and personal growth throughout her years in practice, which include simple things like disconnecting, immersing herself in nature, and being in silence. She suggests asking yourself, "How you can make this an amazing experience?"

The process of saying goodbye is not linear. We may not be able to go back and change a situation that already happened; however, Dr. Ato says, "Your mind is like a file cabinet and when something familiar happens, your mind pulls from the old story to determine how you're going to react in the present. We can change our story."

CONCLUSION

How Do You Know When to Keep Going?

When I first started my virtual assistant business, I wondered how I would know when I should keep going and when I should quit. I'm not a quitter, but sometimes it is the right decision. How would I know what is right for me? Could someone just tell me what to do instead of having to make the decision on my own?

I read stories about wildly successful people who spent their last dime, almost went bankrupt, gave everything they had, and their dreams came true. How did they know? Surely there were people telling them to quit, give up, save what little they had left. I'm sure many of those people were close friends and family members. What makes a person keep going in the midst of hardships? Would I know when to keep going? I've determined there is definitely a time in your business when you know. It's more than a gut feeling.

Certainly, you will have to make changes and improvise along the way. The business I started with is not where I am today. Not everything was worth holding on to. You have to determine if you can get to your end result in another way. It could be that you have to swallow your pride, ask for help, and start all over. None of those things is bad, but they are difficult.

If you are struggling to start your virtual assistant business and wonder how long you should keep going before you quit, ask yourself these two questions:

1. **If I quit now, can I live with my dream never being realized?** Don't feel guilty if the answer is "yes." If you are not all in, it won't work. If it's not your dream, life is too short to spend time on things that don't truly matter to you. Take time to figure out what your real dream is. It may not be business related and that's okay. Sometimes it's your work that supports your dream, not your dream that is the work.

2. **Where is my lack of confidence coming from?** When I wasn't confident, it was all tied to a lack of direction. I didn't understand where I was going and how I was going to get there. I could only see what I wanted the end result to be. Clients can tell when you're not confident, and they want no part of it. Don't confuse a lack of confidence with fear. Fear is a strong emotion so it comes out often, but it still is only a symptom, not the problem. It's possible to fear failure even when you don't know what you're really failing at and quitting.

As a business owner, you'll go through many ups and downs, highs and lows. It could all happen in the same hour. Expect it. Work through it. Then move on. There's no reason you can't be successful. No matter how many virtual assistants there are, there is only one you. What is your gift to the world? If you quit now what would the world be missing out on?

Everything You're Looking for Is Right Around the Corner

Virtual assistant contracts of $60,000 are not often heard of. Especially when so many VAs still charge by the hour. One day I actually sent out two $60,000 contracts. It seemed to happen just like that.

In fact, it was super easy and required almost no effort on my part. I didn't even search for them. Both clients found me through my book *Hire the*

Right Virtual Assistant. No follow-up calls were requested, and there weren't any lengthy processes to complete or hoops to jump through. It was easy because I had already laid the foundation and primed my business. However, I had no idea when I woke up that morning what was waiting for me around the corner.

My first working day in a new country typically had its challenges, and I grew used to many things not going as I had planned them. Having arrived in Morocco only the day before, I can tell you everything was still very new and unfamiliar. I hadn't received my new SIM card, so I couldn't rely on my cell phone for help in this new place. I gave the workspace address to the taxi driver, and off we went.

Driving to new and unfamiliar places is usually exciting and part of the joy of traveling, seeing and experiencing things you never have before. However, the excitement and joy quickly turned to frustration that day when the driver began taking me to several taxi stands to ask for directions. Even with the address, he didn't know where he was going.

After the third stop and rising cab fare, I requested he take me back home. It was the only thing he understood. Up until this point, the frustration in his voice stemmed from the fact I don't speak Arabic or French. Since I didn't have a SIM card, I couldn't use Google Translate either. Now the driver was also frustrated because he did understand that I wasn't going to pay him since he never got me to my destination.

Finally, I arrived back at home. I was no longer frustrated. Now, I was upset and quite shaken. Suddenly I began to realize all that could have gone wrong, and I felt like I escaped some kind of danger. What-ifs flooded my mind, and the adventure of being in a new country had completely disappeared.

I contacted my trip's operations team to let them know what happened and how upset and shaken I was. One of the team members assured me that the city of Rabat is safe. He also told me I was "very close" to my ultimate destination when I asked the taxi driver to turn around.

This information did not comfort me at all. In fact, it did just the opposite. How dare he say such things to me! I didn't know where the location was, so how could I know how close I was? How could I know if the driver was really trying to take me to the right place? Still, I managed to pull myself together and allowed another driver to pick me up and take me to the workspace.

It was then that I saw for myself how close I had been the first time. Now I knew for sure I never was in any real danger. I could get to work and do what I do best.

There were so many "what ifs." What if I let that experience ruin my day and my trip? What if I canceled my appointments for the day? What if I stopped trying and quit? I would have lost out on $120,000! I had no idea how close I was when I woke up that morning.

The same is true in business. Every time you struggle or have a bad day, it may be difficult to believe things can be different. But in reality, each struggle and problem is an opportunity to create a new situation for yourself. What you're looking for is just on the other side.

In 2016, I went on my first international trip. In 2017, I traveled the world—16 countries in 12 months. I didn't know how close I was to living this dream! All of it seemed to happen quickly and unexpectedly, but that's not true. I've done hard work to get me to this place.

If you are looking for your first client, he or she is closer than you think. If you're trying to grow your business, there are more opportunities than you realize. If you want to take a big leap and do something you've never done before, there is a way and it's probably just around the corner. My business coach likes to say, "Success is just around the corner. I just wish someone would stop moving the corner!"

When I think back to every good thing or success that came in my business, they all were unexpected. They usually came after a difficult time, so I should have been expecting good things. I wasn't. I had put in the hard work and made an effort to make things happen. The problem is you don't know when your hard work is going to pay off. You simply have to believe it will.

Could your corner be just as close? Is it time to get to the other side of whatever you want? If you've put in the work, then yes, it's time. I want to read your success story. I want to know what you overcame. More importantly, I want you to know you are closer than you think.

What Will You Be Celebrating in a Year?

As a virtual assistant matchmaker and consultant, one of the best parts of my job is getting to hear about the exciting things my clients are doing. The anticipation in their voices when they speak of the future is undeniable. Immediately I'm going through my list of virtual assistants to find them the perfect match based on communication strategy and ideal client fit.

The tables turned in May 2016. It was an especially exciting time in my world. My book *Hire the Right Virtual Assistant* was released on May 15, 2016, and quickly became an Amazon bestseller. Talking to VAs, clients, and business affiliates about what I was doing, they could hear the anticipation in *my* voice. Since the release of my first book, I have been able to reach and help so many people who I wouldn't have had the opportunity to serve otherwise.

It's been over a year now since I published that book, and I can tell you it was one of the best things I could have ever done for my business. At times

I was terrified of the book flopping. I pressed on because I knew it was necessary to write that book. What I could have never known is how much it would change my life and business. The new areas of growth, new opportunities, and new people I have encountered along the way are direct results of publishing my book.

I thought that was the top of my game. I couldn't imagine a year from then I would be traveling the world and falling in love with Barcelona in May of 2017. What a difference a year makes!

On August 9, 2017, I took a break from work and headed out to the Blue Lagoon in Croatia. The different shades of blue in the water let you know where it is deep and where it is shallow.

While our boat was anchored, our guide pointed to the dock. He encouraged us to jump from the dock, otherwise we couldn't say that we'd really been to this beautiful place. I had no idea if the story was true or not, but I knew I had to do it. I didn't wait for anyone else. I immediately jumped off our boat and started swimming toward the dock. Considering I'm not a great swimmer, you might have thought I would have asked how far the dock was or how long it would take me to swim there. I didn't.

I also seemed to forget the beaches were full of rocks not sand. Getting out of the water was more difficult for me than swimming to the dock. The rocks were extremely slippery, and I had to choose my next steps very carefully. Talk about slippery when wet! I thought of about 100 business metaphors as I made my way over the rocky terrain to the dock. I forgot them all as I stared into the water from on top of the dock.

I didn't realize I would be scared to jump in nor did it make sense. I had already jumped off a boat, swam to the dock, made it over the rocky terrain to get to this point. All I needed to do was jump. This was supposed to be the easy part. It was not at all a long way down, but I was scared and couldn't do it—a far cry from my teenage years when I jumped off cliffs without a care in the world. Of course, the longer I waited, the more fearful I became. Like a little girl, I clenched my fists and made the motions as if I would jump, but I didn't. Then I heard someone shout my name along with instructions.

One of my traveling companions was swimming not too far away and saw me staring into the water from the dock. Like an angel, not to watch over me but to give me permission and strength, she yelled out, "Meeeliissaaa! What are you waiting for? Jump, Meeeliissaaa! Jump!" (You need to say it with a Latina accent to get the full effect.) Her encouragement was unmistakable. There was no need to lift my head to see who was yelling at me. I knew. I leapt off the dock and cannonballed into the water.

Maybe you have gone through all the steps in this book. You made the leap, have done the work, overcame a few obstacles, and there is just one more thing you have to do. But fear has paralyzed you. You know in your heart you're ready, but you just need to hear the voice of someone who believes in you.

I'm here. I believe in you. Send me an email telling me that you're ready to jump, and I'll be that voice of encouragement. If you are my fearless friend already swimming in the water, good for you! The offer still stands, and I relish the opportunity to go through this experience with you.

You can do this.

My wish for you is that you find the joy in the journey, that you step into a life destined to be lived by you alone, and ultimately that you become the VA of the future.

Let me be the first to congratulate you. Congratulations!

ADDITIONAL RESOURCES

"Not all readers are leaders,
but all leaders are readers."

– Harry S. Truman

Below you will find links to the books, articles, websites, and other helpful resources referenced throughout the book. Leaders are, in fact, readers. I encourage you to join the ranks of some of the most successful CEOs in the world by reading these resources. It is estimated that successful CEOs read 60 books every year. Be the best CEO you can and read!

Books

Hire the Right Virtual Assistant: How the Right VA Will Make Your Life Easier, Create Time, and Make You More Money by Melissa Smith, The PVA

Creativity, Inc.: Overcoming the Unseen Forces That Stand in the Way of True Inspiration by Ed Catmull

Profit First: Transform Your Business from a Cash-Eating Monster to a Money-Making Machine by Mike Michalowicz

It's Time to Sell: Cultivating the Sales Mind-set by Chris Spurvey

The Bootstrap VA: The Go-Getter's Guide to Becoming a Virtual Assistant, Getting and Keeping Clients, and More! by Lisa Morosky

Badass Your Brand by Pia Silva

Entrepreneurial You: Monetize Your Expertise, Create Multiple Income Streams, and Thrive by Dorie Clark

Lingo: Discover Your Ideal Customer's Secret Language and Make Your Business Irresistible by Jeffrey Shaw

The Good Goodbye: How to Navigate Change and Loss in Life, Love, and Work by Gladys Ato Psy.D.

Difficult Conversations: How to Discuss What Matters Most by Douglas Stone, Bruce Patton, Sheila Heen

Giftology: The Art and Science of Using Gifts to Cut Through the Noise, Increase Referrals, and Strengthen Retention by John Ruhlin

The E-Myth Revisited: Why Most Small Businesses Don't Work and What to Do About it by Michael E. Gerber

The Best Place to Work: The Art and Science of Creating an Extraordinary Workplace by Ron Friedman PhD

Podcasts

Creative Warriors: www.creativewarriorsunite.com/category/podcast/

Cary Hokama: www.caryhokama.com/blog/

Mixergy: www.mixergy.com

Forms

Ideal Client Avatar Questions:
https://docs.google.com/document/d/15e2no7n8N0T8tAASey8MIIC
ea7ZLuG-6AbsMOulGGO0/edit

Consultation:
https://drive.google.com/file/d/0Byu7P8vJHprNSkh0NVRCTElEV
mM/view

10 Gifts To Avoid Giving Key Clients:
http://giftologybook.com/10-worst-gifts-for-results/

Articles

It's Price Before Product. Period.:
www.firstround.com/review/its-price-before-product-period/

*When We Started Turning Away Clients Our Business Really Took
Off:*
www.forbes.com/sites/piasilva/2017/02/06/when-we-started-turning-
away-clients-our-business-really-took-off/#5f88f85e2192

The 2 Mental Shifts Highly Successful People Make:
www.medium.com/thrive-global/the-2-mental-shifts-every-highly-
successful-person-makes-c757ead99a99

The Art of the Done List: Harnessing the Power of Progress:
www.99u.adobe.com/articles/24875/the-art-of-the-done-list-
harnessing-the-power-of-progress

10 Reasons You Cannot Afford Not To Take A Vacation:
www.forbes.com/sites/tinethygesen/2016/07/08/10-reasons-you-
cannot-afford-not-to-take-a-vacation/#509a7d3d7a0f

Want To Challenge How Much Work Can Be Done Remotely?:
www.thepva.com/want-challenge-much-work-can-done-remotely/

*Survey: People's Trust Has Declined in Business, Media, Government,
and NGOs:*
www.hbr.org/2017/01/survey-peoples-trust-has-declined-in-business-
media-government-and-ngos

Online Classes

Admin to VA Summit: www.admintovasummit.com/

Essential Business Model for Vas :
www.thepva.samcart.com/products/the-essential-business-model-for-vas

Organizations

OrgOrg: www.orgorg.co

OfficeNinjas: www.officeninjas.com

National Association of Women Business Owners (NAWBO): www.nawbo.org/

Websites

Dr. Alvin C. Miles: www.alvincmiles.com

Chris Spurvey: www.chrisspurvey.com

Dorie Clark: www.dorieclark.com

Dr. Gladys Ato: wwwdrgladysato.com

ignite80: www.ignite80.com

Jeffrey Shaw: www.jeffreyshaw.com

Mike Michalowicz: www.mikemichalowicz.com

Pia Silva: www.piasilva.com

Ruhlin Group: www.ruhlingroup.com

Melissa Smith, The PVA

The PVA: www.thepva.com

The Socialista Projects: www.facebook.com/BlogWithMe/

Remote Working Options

Outsite: www.outsite.co

We Roam: www.we-roam.com

Surveys and Statistics

Bureau of Labor Statistics – Administrative Assistant Job Growth Rate:
www.bls.gov/ooh/office-and-administrative-support/secretaries-and-administrative-assistants.htm

The 2016 Deloitte Millennial Survey:
www2.deloitte.com/content/dam/Deloitte/global/Documents/About-Deloitte/gx-millenial-survey-2016-exec-summary.pdf

United States Department of Labor – Federal Internship Compliance:
www.dol.gov/whd/regs/compliance/whdfs71.htm

Global Workplace Analytics:
www.globalworkplaceanalytics.com

FUNDAMENTAL TECHNOLOGY TOOLS

Customer Relationship Management (CRM)

17hats (not technically considered a CRM but often used as one):
www.17hats.com

Contactually: www.contactually.com

Infusionsoft: www.infusionsoft.com

Ontraport: www.ontraport.com

Salesforce: www.salesforce.com

File Sharing

Box: www.box.com

Dropbox: www.dropbox.com

Google Drive: www.google.com/drive/

OneDrive: www.onedrive.live.com/about/en-us/

ShareFile: www.sharefile.com

Newsletters, Email Marketing, and Drip Campaigns

ActiveCampaign: www.activecampaign.com

AWeber: www.aweber.com

Constant Contact: www.constantcontact.com

ConvertKit: www.convertkit.com

MailChimp: www.mailchimp.com

Scheduling Tools

Acuity Scheduling: www.acuityscheduling.com

Calendly: www.calendly.com

Mixmax: www.mixmax.com/calendar

ScheduleOnce: www.scheduleonce.com

Setmore: www.setmore.com

Video Chat

Daily: www.daily.co

Google Hangouts: www.hangouts.google.com

GoToMeeting: www.gotomeeting.com

Skype: www.skype.com/en/

Zoom: www.zoom.us

ACKNOWLEDGEMENTS

Thank you to my family, friends, and colleagues who supported me during my yearlong journey to live and work in 12 countries in 12 months. (I managed to sneak in four more countries!)

To my fellow Polaris Roamers, what a year it was! We were the first! Thank you for the support along the way. From technical to emotional to celebratory, it was a pleasure to break away from work and travel the world with you all. My time would not have been the same without all of you.

To every new, current, and seasoned VA whom I've consulted, you made all this possible. To my pilot class participants of The Essential Business Model for VAs online course, I had a blast! To all the current admins and those who came before me, thank you for making this a profession I fell in love with and am proud to be a part of.

Thank you to all my VAs who have worked with me through the process of writing this book. It's a labor of love, and I thank you for sharing the labor of your own love with me.

To my Recognized Expert mastermind group, thank you for supporting me and pushing me to be my best. I consider myself in great company. I am honored to be the sum of you ladies.

Thank you to all my former bosses, supervisors, department heads, deans, and current clients. You made me better!

To my mom, LaVonne Goldschmidt, CAP-OM, now proudly retired after many years of service, all I ever wanted to be was like you. If I've served half as well as you, I will have made a difference. Thank you for being an example of not only a woman, an assistant, and a leader but a wife and mother as well. Being your daughter is a privilege.

Thank you to my sister, Bambi, and my brother, Joshua, for your support. All the messages, calls, and texts of support were life changing. You're not only my siblings but my best friends. You've given me the gift of three amazing nephews and my precious niece. I work tirelessly to spend as much time with them as my own children.

Lastly, to my children, Isaac and Elyssa, for you both I wish nothing more than to leave a legacy. To show you that you're never too old, it's never too late, and you can have what you dream. Thank you for supporting and championing my goals and dreams.

ABOUT THE AUTHOR

Melissa Smith is The PVA (The Personal Virtual Assistant). As a second generation admin, you'll find that it's in her DNA, and she is passionate about bringing awareness to the world of virtual assistance. When she's not traveling, she calls both California and Georgia home. Melissa makes it a priority to spend time with her children, nephews, and niece on both coasts. The best part of Melissa's virtual work is that it allows her to be location independent. When she's not working, spending time with her family, or traveling, you'll find her cheering on her beloved Virginia Tech Wrestling Hokies.

Made in the USA
Coppell, TX
21 March 2020

17383129R00141